Fran Hill is an English teacher ~~in~~ Warwickshire. Many of her article~~s~~ published in *TES*, *emagazine*, *MsL*~~e~~ ~~technol~~ogies. Her first book about the teaching life, *Being Miss*, was self-published in 2014. Find out more at www.franhill.co.uk.

MISS, WHAT DOES INCOMPREHENSIBLE MEAN?

Fran Hill

First published in Great Britain in 2020

Society for Promoting Christian Knowledge
36 Causton Street
London SW1P 4ST
www.spck.org.uk

British Library Cataloguing-in-Publication Data
A catalogue record for this book is available from the British Library

ISBN 978–0–281–08199–8
eBook ISBN 978–0–281–08200–1

Typeset by Manila Typesetting Company
First printed in Great Britain by Jellyfish Print Solutions
Subsequently digitally reprinted in Great Britain

eBook by Manila Typesetting Company

Produced on paper from sustainable forests

To all those I've taught, and to those who've taught me.
In many cases, you've been one and the same.

Disclaimer

Please think of the events, characters and settings in this book as juggling balls that have been lobbed in the air, coming down in a different formation as composites and rearrangements. This applies particularly, in the interests of discretion, to descriptions of school life. Less juggled, I'm sorry to say, are the book's details of my own life, including my past and its impact on my personality. In fact, I would sue myself for defamation of character if I had the money in the bank.

Contents

First half of autumn term

Monday 4 September

First day back, so teacher training. Classes arrive tomorrow. A tedious day, but we could wear jeans, drink our coffee hot and go to the toilet when we chose. Never look a gift horse.

Stuck in the school hall all day, though – its curtains slouching off the rails.

Adrian Parkes had two cheery headmaster's messages for us – he was not impressed by the summer exam results and wanted to remind us that Ofsted found us mediocre last autumn and would return soon to check we're less mediocre. 'Like the Terminator, they'll be back,' he said. We thought he'd smile, but he didn't. And his comb-over is even less convincing than last term.

George, who's been promoted to head caretaker, updated us on summer improvements. Surprise! English block left until last, hence the drilling and hammering.

At break, nano-squares of flapjack. Cake money clearly went on the refurb.

After break, we learned to operate a fire hydrant, chiefly by learning how not to.

Once we'd mopped up, lunch was a leather-skinned baked potato in the dining hall. Afterwards, watched colleagues levering potato skin out of teeth during looooong graveyard-slot session on planning stimulating lessons. Sunlight playing through the windows increased the agony. My eyelids struggled. Three hours' sleep last night. In bathroom this morning, complained to Mirror, 'Why the angst, the self-doubt, so early in the term?'

It sniggered. 'You're fifty-five, as plump as a cushion and your face is sinking. Any further questions?'

Training finished at 3.15. Stayed in English department office until 6, readying for tomorrow. The room looks as it did last term – our desks piled with books and folders, and the shelves in disarray, poetry beside lit. crit., and Shakespeare by Year 7 novels.

In my classroom, the new cupboards and display boards haven't materialized, and wires hang from my light fittings like spaghetti. Classroom windows painted permanently shut. *Must* report this. Middle-aged women need breezes.

Bussed it home, trying to finish my Anita Shreve novel before the term murders reading time. Ate shepherd's pie with Spouse. He cooked, as he'd come home from gardening at 5.

Spent three hours writing stimulating lesson plans in the study upstairs and watching neighbours drink wine on their patio. Then started this diary at bedtime. Auntie Google says wannabe famous writers should journal. Spouse has bought me a mini-lamp to clip to its pages so I won't disturb him. Not exactly a love gift, but hey.

Tuesday 5 September

In our office at lunchtime. First departmental meeting with Camilla Stent, temporary Head of English and, she told us, Cambridge graduate.

Poor Pam is on long-term sick leave after the stroke.

Camilla couldn't make yesterday. She was on her way back from the Big Apple with friends from Cambridge.

Who calls it the Big Apple?

She wears red shoes and matching nails and refused lovely Sally's lemon drizzle cake, patting an abdomen as flat as a board.

Did I mention she went to Cambridge?

'How old, do you reckon?' I asked Sally later. 'Early thirties?'

Sally said she wasn't sure. 'I bet she jogs in Lycra.'

'You could jog in Lycra.'

'I could,' she said. 'But I wouldn't.'

'Saying no to your lemon drizzle, though,' I said. 'It's just wrong.'

Tuesdays this year will be manic. Five hour-long lessons. But that's next week. Periods 1 and 2 today were 'Orientation' with our forms. Didn't work for new Year 7s, wandering corridors all day in voluminous uniforms, spectacularly un-orientated.

Don't like the look of my Year 8 class list. Have put tricky customers at the front on my seating plan.

My Year 12 English Language A-level class is fourteen-strong. Two boys with a never-does-homework reputation. Three pupils – Olivia, Chloe and Gus – could be sophisticated private-school stock, but attend Beauchamp School instead because their parents read *The Guardian* and champion state education. Made sure to enunciate.

Handed out sheaves of essays to last year's Year 10 class, now Year 11s and facing GCSEs. 'Lovingly marked in purple pen on holiday in Tenby,' I said.

'Did I write this stuff?' one said, flipping the pages as though examining an ancient relic.

Hoped old Year 12, now Year 13 A-level Literature class, would return with more oomph than last term. But 'What homework?' they said.

Rebekah, with glasses and peer contempt, rescued me. 'Miss definitely told us. Look.' She produced a fistful of handwritten notes on her chosen coursework texts.

At least the hammering and drilling have stopped now.

A client gave Spouse a bottle of Baileys Irish Cream today. I poured us both a glass before bedtime. 'Generous measure,' he said, when I passed him his. 'Forgotten Sunday's sermon, then? The spirit is willing, but the flesh is –'

'The flesh is knackered. If you don't want yours, I'll take it back.'

But he did.

Just told Spouse I'm only writing this diary on school days.

'Why?' he said.

'You're always telling me weekends and holidays should be different,' I said.

'I'm talking about your schoolwork leaching into your free time. Actually, not leaching. Flooding.'

'I can't fix that. But I can differentiate them this way. It's a start, isn't it?'

He said I was clutching at straws and turned off his lamp.

Wednesday 6 September

Late night Baileys: my new best friend. Six hours' sleep!

At school, George poked his flat-capped head round my classroom door before registration to check that the lights had been sorted.

'Spaghetti all gone,' I said, then had to explain.

When he'd left, I realized I'd forgotten to mention the windows. And it's been a warm day. 'The windows are painted shut,' I explained to my Year 11 form in registration. 'Stop chatting, or we'll use up the oxygen and die as one.'

Spent most of Period 1 – my 'free' period – finding out that we must email caretaking requests now rather than phone their office. There's been a restructure. Was sent an email ticket numbered 301.

Year 12 want to sit in rows despite a school-wide push to seat sixth-formers in 'shapes'. 'What about a horseshoe formation?' I said. No takers.

Gus wanted to know if we'd be studying Anglo-Saxon inflections as part of the course.

'*Pff.* Thankfully not!' I said.

'Oh, I see.' He sounded like someone who's ordered caviar and quinoa with a blackcurrant reduction and got a stale Cornish pasty. I clobbered them with some grammar to even things up a bit.

Ingredients of Year 13 class: the half interested, two definite weed-smokers, and Rebekah with her condescension towards the rest of humankind. They are mostly, at best, 'meh' about studying *The Handmaid's Tale*. Nevertheless, we started with Atwood's use of biblical references today.

Rebekah says her parents named her after the Bible's Rebekah, the one who married Isaac. Rebekah definitely knows her Bible stories. The others hadn't a clue. Conor thought a Testament was a body part.

Rebekah had to leave early for an orchestra rehearsal. She plays flute, cello and piano. Of course she does.

Another free period at the end of the day. Was collecting resources for *Handmaid* in the English office when Camilla came in. We are teaching the same sixth-form classes, splitting the courses between us. She'd spotted the Year 12s seated in rows in my lesson and wished to tell me that she favours shapes.

Bussed it to Wednesday Bible study group at Jean's home with Spouse. They discussed Sunday's sermon about the flesh.

Stayed quiet.

Thursday 7 September

Whoever makes Baileys, surely two nights in a row wasn't much to ask?

Taught about the dangers of alcohol in the Thursday morning Personal, Health, Social and Economic Education lesson with my Year 11 form. (Diary, don't expect to get that written out in full ever again.) Felt guilty about the Baileys – had half a tumbler last night. Slippery slope and all that.

What if the pupils knew what I'm really like? And what I was like at their age.

Asked Year 7 to write about their summer experiences in our first lesson. Not one went to Tenby. More like Spain, the Canaries, Greece. Since when was a week in Margate not enough for people?

Told them we'd be studying poetry forms this half-term, focusing on ballads. 'Ballads are mostly about tragic deaths,' I said, cheerfully. 'Welcome to secondary school English.'

One girl blanched. I felt a bit less jealous of her fortnight in Morocco.

First-rate new teaching assistant, Lynne, there to support two Year 7s in particular, but she'll be a boon. Tiny woman with elfin haircut and a massive heart. She's in my Year 8 class too. Yay!

Spouse told me this evening over curry that he's started power walking.

Asked him how that was different from all his other walking. 'You're always out walking.'

'It's not "strolling in the fields looking at sheep" walking. It's about getting your heart rate up.'

'Jogging?'

'You know I can't jog. Not with gardener's knees.'

I said it was late for a midlife crisis.

'I'm only sixty-one,' he said. 'Anyway, you could come with me.'

Told him I'd pass on that, and could he power walk to the kitchen and wash up? I pointed to the pile of Year 7 books on the dining table. 'Thirty-two to mark. A fun evening ahead.'

'Power walks will keep me fit,' he said.

'You're a gardener.'

'That's work.'

Gathered the pile of books to take to the study and said I supposed it was better than a motorbike and a blonde. 'You're not shaving your beard off, are you?'

'Look,' he said, picking up our plates. 'My mum's frail. My dad died before he should've. I want to make sure I don't.'

Felt bad. Marked Year 7 books until 11.30 p.m. and felt better.

Friday 8 September

Found a curry stain on a Year 7's exercise book. It *would* be a child with copperplate handwriting and doubtless copperplate parents. Glad it happened in Week 1, while she's still too petrified to query it.

Furious spot on chin. I said to Mirror, 'What do you call *this*?'

'Vesuvius?' it said.

Not sure my tube of spot concealer will last the week, let alone the term.

Auntie Google says menopause can revive acne, normally a feature of adolescence. So, where are the pert breasts too? The clear eyes? Eating chips for seven nights without ill effect?

Friday break duty this year. Unfair. It's the only day there's cake in the staffroom. Stood there checking uniforms. They're already going to seed. I said, 'Tuck it in, please,' thirty-nine times. At least the weather's moderate. September break duty on a corridor can braise you alive.

The Year 9s I share with Jim Jones seem biddable. Will only teach them once a week. Started off with a spelling test to endear myself.

Pursued the grammar with Year 12. Only the Privates understand what a subordinate clause is. The others can't even identify a verb. It's like a horse race in which the winning steeds have five legs and the rest three.

Year 8 still surprisingly tame during Period 5. 'Honeymoon,' Lynne said. Started class novel, *A Monster Calls* by Patrick Ness. Asked the class if they had any recurring dreams like the main character does.

Won't do that again.

Sally's teaching the same novel. She said thanks for the tips on activities to avoid.

Camilla works in her classroom after school, not in the English office. Maybe she's afraid of contamination. Jim, who's Welsh and honest, and has been a teacher for a hundred years, said he wouldn't lose sleep over it.

'I have insomnia,' I told him. 'It's my age.'

'So does my wife. We're in separate rooms.'

Oh.

Camilla has a livid scar on her forehead, under her fringe. She told Sally she was in a car crash last summer.

Finished Anita Shreve on the bus.

Seeing the family for lunch on Saturday. Better get quality time with Son, Daughter-in-law and the two Littluns before schoolwork takes over weekends.

Resisted Baileys tonight. I'm on the rota to lead worship at church on Sunday. My singing and guitar-playing never was Lady Gaga, but I'm sure I'm losing my edge. Substance abuse won't help matters.

Monday 11 September

Saturday afternoon was relaxing, playing snap with Grandboy and Grandgirl. Almost as good as Baileys.

For five and three, they're quick on the draw. Too quick for me. I've been fast-forwarded into the autumn of my life. 'Do you mind that I don't knit?' I asked my daughter-in-law.

Said to Spouse later that they probably prefer GapKids clothes anyway. But Spouse said a home-knit cardi costs a fiver – a pair of GapKids pyjamas might bankrupt us.

'The young have different tastes,' I said.

'The young have debts,' he said.

Good news: free period first thing on Mondays this year. Spent today's in a photocopier queue, waiting for two engineers to mend the machines. I could have come back later, but one engineer looked like Sean Bean.

Double Year 11 before lunch – not the ideal hors d'oeuvre. Danny stood up while I was talking and peered over my left shoulder. 'Pizza and apple crumble!' he announced, reading from the weekly lunch menu pinned up behind me.

'Forgive me for blocking your view, Danny,' I said, 'while trying to educate you.'

He said sorry, but he was starving and not thinking straight. I know he plays rugby, but – built like a shed with a head, even at fifteen?

I thought I'd ask the class how many had read a book for pleasure in the holidays. Four out of thirty! No wonder they still say 'brought' when they mean 'bought'.

The Year 7s, studying poetry forms in Period 5, wrote haiku. One reads,

I want to go sleep
My eyes are very heavy
When will the bell go?

Delighted to have inspired them.

Lynne says she might apply for teacher training next year. She's not sure. 'Isn't thirty-eight too old?' she said.

Told her I'd trained at forty.

She asked why I wasn't a Head of Department by now.

'I trained to teach,' I said, 'not manage people, and I'd had enough of futile paperwork in the NHS.'

'Plus,' she said, 'you can go to department socials without feeling like a pariah.'

Spouse out for an hour before dinner tonight. Came back sweaty and needing a shower, so I put the fish pie on hold and it shrivelled up.

Conked out on sofa later. When I woke up, he'd gone to bed.

Must set haiku more often. Marked thirty-two books in an hour.

Tuesday 12 September

'Was my mouth hanging open when I fell asleep last night?' I asked Spouse this morning in the kitchen.

He said he couldn't possibly comment but he'd been tempted to feed me a watermelon.

I said to Mirror, 'What if Spouse gets fit and lithe and loses the paunch? We won't match any more.'

Arrived in my classroom after Adrian's lugubrious Tuesday morning briefing to staff. Found George inspecting the painted-over windows. He said, 'A load of muppets, that's what they are.'

'It's a good thing the weather's cooler,' I said. 'I don't need more help to have a hot flush.'

Apparently, I'd get on with his wife, who can rip off a cardigan in 1.6 seconds.

I'm teaching *A Monster Calls* to Year 8 and *An Inspector Calls* to Year 11. Might write my own story – *Nature Calls* – about a menopausal woman. The literary canon needs a bit of shaking up.

In our lunchtime meeting, Camilla said that the senior management team (I bet she'll never call them the Smuts like we do) wants a volunteer English teacher to produce a new school magazine.

We all looked at fluff on the carpet.

Told the others when she'd gone, 'If anyone squeaks that I produced my last school's magazine . . .'

I hear they found a fatberg in an east London sewer today the size of eleven buses. How did it start? Probably a wet wipe and some chip fat down a sink in Waltham Forest. My marking load's the same. Suddenly out of control. Carried Year 11 essays, Year 13 coursework proposals and Year 8 classwork home today, bent under the weight of my rucksack like a Sherpa. Mostly, *je ne regrette rien* about ditching our car for public transport and legs and Spouse's bicycle. Today, *je regrette* shedloads.

Marked three Year 8 books, then Spouse yelled upstairs, 'Did you remember the theatre?'

'Yup. Just getting jeans on,' I called back, and tiptoed into the bedroom.

A decent am-dram production of *The Importance of Being Earnest*. A relief to watch other people's confused lives and mindlessly stuff down enough Revels to feed the West Midlands.

Wednesday 13 September

Started marking coursework proposals in Period 1, hoping to finish them by the lesson. Slight hitch. Bahlul is free then too and loves to chat. He swears people in Libya chat more than Brits.

Bahlul's particular skill set: avoiding work.

Year 13 will have to wait to get their proposals back.

No progress on display boards, cupboards or stuck windows. A Year 11 pupil pulled an inhaler out this morning and feigned lack of breath. At least, I hope she feigned. Complained to Camilla, but classroom fixtures and fittings not her 'area'.

Year 12 are learning about how new words enter our language. Today: culinary terms. An argument broke out. Why are foreign words like 'pizza', 'paella' and 'sushi' called 'borrowings', they wanted to know? Why not 'stealings'? When did we plan to return them? Then they insisted on making a list of such foodie words. The bell went on number 173, 'kimchi'.

That's what happens when people let teenagers watch *Masterchef* and eat in proper restaurants on Fridays. It should be stopped.

Trudged home at 9 p.m. after an information meeting for Year 11 parents. The parents had swooped like vultures during wine and nibbles.

'She's very anxious.'

'Can you help him with his handwriting?'

'Make sure he doesn't sit near Ben, Jake or Ed.'

Never mind all that, I wanted to say. *Please drag them off Instagram and force them to read a pigging book.*

Spouse went to Bible study at Jean's. 'Make sure they know I have a compulsory meeting,' I had told him this morning.

Avoided the Baileys and felt a bit more Christian, even without Bible study.

Thursday 14 September

Only one spot, but it's *plumb* in the middle of my forehead, as though I've been shot.

In better news, display boards arrived on my classroom walls overnight. But Camilla wants them covered in students' work immediately. Apparently, a parent-governor is touring the school tomorrow and needs impressing. 'I could show him this forehead spot,' I told Sally. 'That's impressive. Even under the concealer.'

'I get those,' she said.

I told her I'd never seen them.

She said, 'You don't notice my spots, just as I don't notice yours, you idiot.'

Tempted to ask Year 8s to illustrate their recurring dreams for the display boards. Sally said, 'Go ahead. I believe Asda are recruiting.'

Hid myself in the library's darkest corner during free period to conquer some marking. Begged the librarian, 'If anyone asks, you haven't seen me. If it's emergency cover in science, you've never even *heard* of me.'

Camilla's sent falsely cheerful email re school magazine. 'A little bird says you've had articles published,' she wrote. 'Dark horse, you! Let's chat.'

If I catch that little bird, I'll wring its birdy little neck.

Dabbed spots with toothpaste at bedtime. Auntie Google advises it. Got into bed to write diary and told Spouse, 'Don't kiss me until it's dried,' but he fell asleep while I was still tacky.

More power walking this evening. I thought it might be a temporary fad. Maybe there *is* a blonde.

Friday 15 September

Toothpaste dries like concrete. Had to scrub it so hard this morning I cancelled out healing work done in the night.

Sunny September morning. I should have walked. It's only forty minutes. But (a) my school rucksack is always too heavy and (b) Spouse is clearly walking enough for both of us.

Camilla butted in on my Year 7 lesson as I was setting homework. '*Where* will we find a sonnet from a modern poet?' the pupils had whined while copying the instruction from the whiteboard.

I was saying, 'Well, at the end of this corridor, there's this thing called a *library*,' when Camilla clacked in, all heels and haughtiness. Other colleagues would knock.

She was checking the display boards. I'd pinned up Year 7 haiku, omitting the one about heavy eyes. Not a professional display, but if I'd had a talent for displays, I'd have become a window dresser.

'Very good,' she said, and clacked out again.

A Year 7 girl asked, 'Was that lady an inspector, Miss?'

I said, 'Yes, in a way.'

Spouse is visiting his mother in Twickenham this weekend, leaving me to my schoolwork. 'She might not be here this time next year,' he said, 'and I'll go and see the girls in Isleworth.'

Visiting our two daughters without me?

He called a taxi. 'There's a train from Leamington in half an hour.'

'But there's been a bomb at Parson's Green this morning,' I said at the door.

He kissed me. 'It's Twickenham. Nowhere near the centre. We used to live there, remember? You've got neurotic now we're in the sticks.'

Went a bit crazy with the Baileys when he'd gone. But it's 2 a.m. now and here I am, sleepless and writing this.

No need for the clip-on light, at least.

Monday 18 September

Spouse arrived back late. I was asleep, dreaming his blonde was Sally.

I woke at 6 a.m. He was still asleep.

If you only see your loved ones with their mouths hanging open, surely things are slipping.

Two purple pens down after the weekend. Laid them in empty wastepaper basket so Spouse would see.

Hid in the library during Period 1 to plan lessons. But Bahlul brought in his Year 7s for quiet reading. Whoever had the bright idea to put bean bags in libraries for fidgety eleven-year-olds should be shot at dawn.

He came over. 'Sorry if I've dobbed you in to Camilla.'

He's the little birdy. I knew it.

'Published in *TES*, though!' he said. 'I'd tell everyone!'

'Please say you didn't tell her that. It's a while ago, anyway, since I wrote for them.'

'What's the problem?' he said. 'It's a national. She could have read you for herself.'

'Had she, though?' I asked him.

He said no. Not until he'd sent her the web link.

He slunk off back to his rustling Year 7s.

My Year 8 front row is warming up. Gave two detentions. Typed their offences and sanctions into the school information management system, choosing my words carefully now that the Smuts let parents log on to SIMS and read the comments.

Be my guest, Mums and Dads, and while you're here, have my credit card numbers and this photograph of my sock drawer.

An email from Camilla: 'Can we meet Wednesday lunchtime to discuss magazines and sixth-formers?'

I have new classroom cupboards. Nothing like the old 1950s oak and reliable ones. These are grey metal, sourced from Furniture Suppliers to Schools and Prisons.

Year 11 think I should write another version of *An Inspector Calls* featuring Ofsted. With 'scary scenes'. I swear we're making a whole generation of schoolkids paranoid.

'The Ballad of Charlotte Dymond' is alarming some flaky Year 7s. One said she's having nightmares.

Best not use the PowerPoint with the dripping blood graphic.

Fell in the door after school and asked Spouse how his mum was.

'Fine. Feeling stronger. She wanted to know all about the power walking.'

Is that a dig? I nearly said. But he'd cooked tarragon chicken and roasted sweet potatoes. 'How were the girls?' I said instead.

'Both well. We all had a takeaway at theirs.'

'Oh.'

He was whistling as he laced his trainers this evening.

Tuesday 19 September

Spot-free face, save a pink patch on my forehead where last week's mega-spot sat. I look like a Hindu who's left the faith.

Adrian's Tuesday briefing wasn't brief enough. And if you're dragging staff from vital photocopying and prep merely to lecture and chip away at self-esteem, a smile doesn't go amiss.

Told Year 7 that, on the basis of their homework, today's lesson would be literacy.

'We thought we were doing ballads,' they said.

'And I thought you'd know what a paragraph was,' I said. 'That's all of us disappointed, then.'

Lynne looked disapproving of the sarcasm, so I added, 'But, as always, I'm here to help.'

The two Year 8 detention boys weren't chuffed about completing a new form I've designed. Shame. I was pleased with it myself, especially the questions 'What did I do to end up here?' and 'How can I avoid coming again?'

I bit into my flapjack. 'Mmm, lovely,' I said to the boys, crumbs cascading on to my lap as Camilla walked in to fetch a book she'd left on my desk.

'Are we still lunching tomorrow?' I asked her.

She looked down at the crumbed carpet and back up at my flapjack as if to say, *If you eat cakes the size of breeze blocks at break, will you need lunch?* I waited for her to reply/smile/ask how I was, but she turned and left.

They waited for Godot in the same way.

Introduced Year 12 to the work of the linguist David Crystal. 'He's my guru,' I said. 'When I say his name in lessons, you must bow your heads and say, "O blessed be his holy name."' I made them practise.

Chloe said to Olivia, 'I never know whether she's being serious; that's the trouble.'

Booked a computer room in Period 5 so Year 13 could start drafting coursework. What a shambles. Only Rebekah brought everything she needed.

We need a new bottle of Baileys. I'm waiting for Spouse to suggest it.

Wednesday 20 September

Met Sally coming down the English office stairs as I returned from registration. She stopped. 'Is that the Departmental Plan?' she said, nodding towards the thick document Camilla gave us each at Tuesday lunchtime's meeting. It was under my arm.

'Skimmed it,' I said. 'On the bus. In between swigs from a hip flask.'

'Busy year coming up. It's not like anything else is happening.'

I asked her to remind me when her wedding was.

'I meant Ofsted,' she said. 'But July. First day of the hols.'

Two Year 8 girls I hadn't noticed near the stairwell screeched, 'Wedding? You're getting married, Miss?' and skittered off to tell the whole universe.

'Oops,' I said.

'Ah well,' Sally said. 'Better out than in, maybe.'

'Like pus?' I said.

'Like pus? Do you *want* to be invited?'

Menopausal spots are taking over my thought processes.

'Although,' she said, 'if I can't stop Archie spending all our savings, we'll be having a budget wedding and no one will be invited.'

Lunch with Camilla. Me: beef stew and lumpy mash. Her: three pieces of cucumber. She relayed begging message from Adrian re magazine. Felt obliged to agree I'd think about it. I'm not doing it though.

Also discussed division of labour for shared sixth-form classes, aka Camilla handed me a completed Excel spreadsheet.

In my free period, marked Year 8 writing on *A Monster Calls* and a couple of Year 11 homework essays.

Home after Bible study, Spouse said, 'Surprise!' and pulled a bottle of Baileys from a bag.

'Oh!' I said. 'Had we run out?'

Thursday 21 September

Year 11 assembly and Adrian tried to inspire with stories about his statistician career, boring them skull-less except that he was practically eating the microphone. Each time he said 's' it sounded like someone sweeping up leaves. It wouldn't have been half as entertaining had he been a geographer.

Year 11 did well to act out the scene from *An Inspector Calls* today despite unusual background sound effects. Maintenance man stood on ladder throughout the lesson carving open my windows with a Stanley knife and swearing under his breath, and sometimes over it.

Moved off alcohol in PHSE. Now on STIs Part 1. The lesson went astray when I mentioned that my previous career as a medical secretary meant I could write all the difficult words – gonorrhoea, syphilis, genital herpes – in shorthand.

'What's shorthand?' they said.

Demonstrated a few strokes on the whiteboard. 'This is "t". This is "d".' Then wrote 'syphilis' and 'herpes'.

'Can you show us our names in shorthand?' someone said.

We ran over and chlamydia got postponed until Part 2.

Bahlul's forty-second birthday. He'd brought in sweet pastries and had no intention of spoiling his day by working. In my free period, I tried to check Year 11's PHSE exercise books with one ear on his chatter and one hand in the bag of pastries. They hadn't written much in the lesson, unless you count beginner's shorthand.

Reached our street at 7 p.m. to see the back of Spouse in the distance, powering away along the pavement, his arms swinging. He'd left a note on the kitchen worktop: 'Stir fry in wok. You carry on.'

Friday 22 September

Tossed and turned last night, trapped in the library with Bahlul. Spouse threw back the covers at 3 a.m. and stomped to the spare room. 'It's like sleeping with a dying fish.'

Said to Mirror at 6 a.m., 'I'm glad you're not a magnifier. These eye bags would look gross.'

Awkward silence.

Grovelling email from Adrian. 'I hear through the grapevine blah blah. You'd be given our full support blah. You would be helping the school enormously blah blah blah.' He said the deadline for the magazine would be halfway through summer term.

Who knew? 'Deadline' originates from prison camps in the American Civil War – a physical boundary beyond which, if you dared cross it, you'd be shot.

Said to Sally, 'I'm telling Year 12 that when I take in their homework.'

She said, 'No, you're not. They're on a Find-Your-Inner-Self motivational day.'

Oh, that old trick. Writing down the homework deadline like innocents, but knowing they wouldn't be in lessons. Even the Privates didn't own up. Hope they find racking guilt in their inner selves.

Told the Jim/me Year 9 class about the deadline thing, to get it off my chest.

Lunchtime clubs started today. Five pitched up for my Senior Writing Club in a computer room during First Lunch. Three Year 10s and two Year 11s. I asked about their motivations for writing. They said there was air conditioning in the computer room in the summer and it was cosy in the winter. But they set to, describing a summer location.

I cling to hope.

Camilla asked me afterwards, as casual as chips, 'Any budding journalists?'

Nine Year 8s had forgotten their books for the Reading lesson, including most of the front row. 'Can we read French textbooks instead,' they said, 'for our test?'

'No,' I said, giving out copies of *Nineteenth Century Short Stories* from the prison cupboard.

Home at 7. Lift from colleague, who shouted, 'Oi, bag lady!' out of her car window. 'What's in all those?' she said. 'Bodies of Year 8s?'

'I wish,' I said. 'I could bury them and have a normal weekend.'

'It's all marking? Seriously?'

'Seriously.'

She teaches IT. Bless.

Babysat for Son and DIL tonight. Read the Littluns *Burglar Bill* and soothed myself to sleep. Didn't have the same effect on them, unfortunately.

Monday 25 September

Skived off church yesterday and sat in garden to mark Year 11 essays on Mr Birling's character in *An Inspector Calls*. A cheerful sun tricked me into early optimism, but most of the class hadn't got him at all. Shockingly flawed understanding evident by essay five, with twenty-five still to go.

Asked God to release me from the teaching profession. So at least I squeezed a prayer in. That must count.

'Do you think I should go back to being a medical secretary?' I said to Spouse on his return.

He spent an hour cooking a risotto so generous we could have invited the British Army round and had baskets of leftovers, like Jesus did with the bread and fish. (Linking everyday events to biblical references surely counts too.)

Email from Camilla this morning. Had I made a decision?

Found her in her classroom, putting lipstick on. She looked embarrassed. She doesn't like surprise conversation.

'I don't know where I'd fit in all the extra work,' I said. 'Are you sure there's no one else?'

'No one as qualified as you,' she said. 'You are ideally suited to this.'

How does she know? We're not exactly conjoined twins.

'I was impressed with your *TES* articles,' she said. 'What a talented writer. The school's lucky to have you.'

Sometimes, I really get why Eve bit that apple.

Year 8 group discussion on *A Monster Calls* disrupted by three girls verbally scratching each other's eyes out. I marched them into the corridor, asking Lynne to watch the rest.

'What's going on?' I said.

The grievance? One, a tall girl with long black hair, has turned thirteen, so is now legally able to use Instagram. The others are still twelve.

'She's goating over us,' one complained, pointing viciously. 'Goating, goating, goating,' she spat.

'Yes, goating,' repeated the other.

'You mean gloating,' said the thirteen-year-old, in possession of both Instagram and a superior vocabulary.

'She's still doing it,' wailed the others.

Separated the three and foisted them on to other groups. Gave the girls detentions for disruption. 'Tomorrow, Second Lunch,' I told them.

At home, I cooked gammon, potatoes and peas while Spouse was out getting his heart rate up.

'Why did I book their detention for Second Lunch?' I said later, mid-potato. 'It's the department meeting.'

'I have no idea what you're talking about,' Spouse said. 'You are asking me questions I have no hope of answering.'

Spouse popped round to Son's for a chat. I unearthed a forgotten bottle of Pinot while he was out. Freezered it for ten minutes to cool it.

Well, 6.5 minutes.

Tuesday 26 September

Spouse slid into bed at 10.30 last night and leaned over to kiss me. Note to self: time the Pinot burps better.

This morning, another furious spot brewing, under my chin. Mirror said, 'It's no good dipping your head like that to hide it. That accentuates your jowls.'

I stuck my tongue out.

'That's childish,' it said.

More fabulous innovation from Adrian announced in briefing. Half-termly assessment grades to parents from now on, not termly, and now we must grade pupils on six different categories: effort, attainment, organization, attitude, class contribution, overall progress.

Why not add quality of pencil case, perpendicularity of arm-raising and use of ruler while underlining date? Arrangement of legs under desk?

Pronunciation of 'scone'?

Told the goating Year 8 and her friends the detention would be tomorrow break instead. 'I have a detention with history tomorrow,' said Goater.

'Thursday, then. That's my final offer,' I said.

Lunchtime department meeting. Camilla's introduced a new weekly slot, sick-bucketly called 'Top Tips for the Team'. We'll all get a slot. She's doing the first six weeks, though, and started today with strategies to help reduce the marking load.

I have to say, regretfully, it was quite useful.

She collared me afterwards. 'How are you feeling about the magazine now?'

Said I'd decide by the end of the week.

'Thursday?' she said.

Haggling?

'Friday morning,' I said. She was looking at my chin. I dipped my head, risking jowlage.

George came into my classroom while I was browsing through Year 12's (late) homework. 'Thought I'd check your windows. Ah. They're open. About time too.'

'I don't have to give out breathing apparatus any more,' I said.

It was Beauchamp's open evening from 4 till 7 p.m. That's a *lot* of compulsory smiling.

At home, shared the rest of the Pinot with Spouse. One glass each. Not a wild night.

Wednesday 27 September

Spent two hours last night downstairs, wrapped in the spare-bed duvet, making notes on *The Handmaid's Tale*, chapters 5–9. Sleep is meant to be healing, so no wonder the chin spot has protested under the concealer all day, in the same way muggers continue to thrash despite being lain on by three burly policemen.

It's as well I'd prepared for Year 13. First period free hijacked by Camilla asking me to cover Jim's class. He found his dog dead in its basket this morning.

Jim's Year 11s turn out to have a detailed, insightful knowledge of Mr Birling. What am I doing wrong with my own Year 11s?

In my Year 13 class, one of the weed-smokers, Matt, smelt suspicious and seemed only half there. Took him outside the classroom and said I'd need to report it to his Head of Year. I tried to sound authoritative. He's well over six feet and I was addressing his nipple area. 'I'm sure your Head of Year will be most disappointed,' I said.

'Like, whatevs,' he said.

I mean, where's the fear?

He followed me back into the classroom.

'What was that all about, Miss?' asked his friend, Conor, another weeder, I suspect.

'Matt's coursework,' I said. Confidentiality and all that.

'The ganja,' Matt said.

Rebekah's contributions to the lessons leave some of the others blinking. She'd prepped today's chapters in as much detail as I had. Was relieved that I'd done it. Insomnia, you're not all bad.

Bible study was about harmony. Awkward, as Spouse and I had had a hissed conflab about the magazine dilemma on the way there on the bus. He said, 'You're going to do it, aren't you? Even though you know you'll regret it.'

Thursday 28 September

The toothpaste trick worked last night. The spot hasn't gone, but pulsates less. Like when a lion attacks you, but only nibbles round the edges. Or a semi-detached house falls on you, but only on your right leg.

Went into school early to arrange National Poetry Day display with Sally on the English corridor. She was telling me about honeymoon plans. (Archie says the Caribbean. She says Ireland.) Because I wasn't concentrating I staple gunned my finger sticking up a war poem.

Sally fetched the First Aid box once she'd stopped laughing.

School photographer in, so Year 11 assembly and PHSE both cancelled. (Laters, chlamydia!) Found my classroom computer equipment unplugged and some hair straighteners warming up during registration. Gave the culprit a telling-off and a lecture about why a school photograph wasn't the Paris catwalk.

Hair straighteners look like the speculums they use for cervical smears. Should I tell her this?

While supervising Goater's detention, drafted a surrender email to Camilla.

Goater filled in my form. 'You've done that very neatly,' I said.

She looked surprised. 'Thanks, Miss. My mum says my writing is terrible.'

Camilla spotted my clumsily applied finger plaster. All she said was, 'Did you fill in an incident report?'

Was almost overwhelmed by her compassion.

Sally brought jam tarts today to cheer Jim up. We gathered round the tin in the office after lunch.

'RIP, Dog,' Jim said.

I asked what the dog's name had been.

'Dog,' he said, biting into a jam tart. 'Cardiff people don't mess about.'

Zak in Year 7 is a problem – restless and a nuisance to anyone he sits next to. Moving him around makes no difference. Currently his neighbour is an angel child, with blonde hair and a bright future. 'I can't concentrate, Miss,' she said today. 'Zak passes me rude notes.'

Zak laughed behind his hand. Gave him a warning, but he seemed unbothered.

'Twilight' teacher training after school from 3.30 to 5 p.m. Teacher from Science department delivered PowerPoint on how to run effective group work, meanwhile putting us in groups and leaving us clueless as to why.

Friday 29 September

No appreciative reply from Camilla to my email. Kept checking for it. Then Jim told me she was on a training day.

Teaching Year 7 in Period 1 was like taming popping candy. Tonight is their school disco.

'Are you coming, Miss?' they squealed.

'Yes,' I said. 'I volunteered to supervise. Call it self-harm.'

Lynne shook her head as if to say, *You're not allowed to say that.*

Higher pitch from Year 7. 'What are you wearing?'

Told them I was dressing down in my sequinned ballgown, gold slippers and a tiara.

They screeched, 'Cool!'

Boring break duty. Yearned for crisp packet littering or someone shouting obscenities in the corridors. Sally brought me coffee from the staffroom machine and some Victoria sponge. She says she'll do so every Friday.

'You don't need to do that,' I said.

'I know I don't,' she said.

Year 12 studying graphology. They learned some specialist vocabulary today. By 'learned' I mean the Privates re-learned, having already memorized the glossary. The rest learned. By 'learned' I mean noted down dutifully, then got 3 out of 15 in the test.

At lunchtime, my Writing Club wrote about ambitions. One wants to be a Kardashian. I said that was very ambitious indeed, considering she was born a Simpkins in Hampton Magna.

Only one Year 8 forgot her reading book this week, but she's a sweet kid who laughs at my jokes. I passed her *The Secret Garden* under the desk.

Seventeen Year 7s bounced up to me tonight at various points, high on Haribo and fizz, to ask why I was wearing jeans and where was my tiara?

'How was it?' Spouse asked me woozily when I climbed into bed and picked up this diary.

Told him that medieval painters who depicted hell must have been to Year 7 discos.

Monday 2 October

Year 11 form sombre today. The shooting at a concert in Las Vegas has unsettled them. They looked at me for help, like abandoned puppies, as though I'd have answers.

Started Act 3 of *Inspector* with Year 11 English class. The natural thespians are coming through. Jake, usually disruptive, is playing Eric like a pro, getting the drunken slurred consonants far too convincingly. 'Are you doing Theatre Studies for GCSE?' I asked him.

'You're joking,' he said. 'I'd get Mr Vinnicombe. I'm doing PE instead.'

'But you're talented.'

He shook his head.

'You are.'

'I know,' he said. 'I was still thinking about Vinnicombe.'

The responsibility. It's terrifying. How many talented writers have I turned into cooks or plumbers?

Sally said later, 'Don't be absurd.'

At least Year 11 seemed more clued up on Mr Birling today. I will stop Googling 'Medical Secretaries Warwick'.

Camilla's delayed reply to my email was a list of emojis: thumbs-ups, hearts, champagne glasses, grinning dogs. I felt nauseous.

Said to Spouse this evening while we ate a beef casserole he'd cooked, 'You are now talking to a magazine editor.'

He said, 'No, I am talking to myself, and have been for weeks.'

A bit harsh.

Rejection email from health magazine. 'Thank you for your piece on menopausal acne. Unfortunately, we only take this kind of article from experts.'

Pff. An expert with an English rose complexion and an NVQ in eyebrow shaping? What about the real experts? Those with foreheads like pizzas and shares in Clearasil?

Tuesday 3 October

Didn't get to sleep until 2 a.m. last night. Couldn't stop thinking about Las Vegas and wished I hadn't clicked on the news video before bedtime.

Year 8 wanted to tell tragic stories about relatives with terminal diseases, like the mother in *A Monster Calls.* Then they moved on to pets. The lesson plan went AWOL. But even the front row was transfixed. 'Can we do that again?' one of them said as we packed up. 'It was well fun.'

Gave Year 12 a practice question on graphology, but the photocopying lady had sliced off the left-hand margin of the exam paper, so the first two letters on every line were missing. Spent ten minutes dictating, so the class could fill them in. Had to avoid the Privates' censorious faces.

Rumours abound in the staffroom that Adrian is considering a Mocksted. It was busy at break, more staff than usual drinking coffee on the low foam chairs with stuffing poking out or surreptitiously browsing jobs in *TES*. The main topic of conversation: why do we need a practice Ofsted inspection run by sneery education consultants? Why line their pockets?

I didn't realize the Head of Science *knew* all those swearwords.

I preface everything I say to Year 13 these days with 'Not you, Rebekah, but . . .'. Today it was 'Not you, Rebekah, but are you all aware that the word "work" appears as part of the word "coursework"?'

Camilla Top Tips #2 in today's department meeting. She's been irritatingly useful two weeks in a row now. I used her highlighting method when marking this evening. Saved enough time to share a bottle of red with Spouse afterwards while we listened to a podcast about middle-aged drinkers.

Wednesday 4 October

Slept like a Calpolled baby.

'That'll be the red wine,' said Mirror.

I also have two spots on my face.

'That'll be the red –'

'OK, *enough*,' I said.

Bahlul off sick, so I got plenty done in my free period.

Some of Year 12 hassled for another half-hour for their practice question, bearing in mind the margin disaster of yesterday and the 'stress and trauma' caused.

That made me cross. 'Stress and trauma? Tell the people of Las Vegas that.'

They went quiet. Bet the Privates dob me in. Now awaiting email from Head of Year 12 about sensitive use of language.

Year 13 are meant to read ahead to save time in class. I'd set them chapters 10–14 of *Handmaid* for the weekend. Matt had done zilch.

'You won't understand the lesson,' I said.

He shrugged. If that boy shrugs any more often, he'll end up with loose shoulder blades and a concertina neck. But perhaps I shouldn't have told him that.

Tonight's Bible study was about controlling the tongue and not speaking impulsively. There are twenty-seven Bible verses about it and we read them all. One by one. Like little pokes with a sharp stick.

I think the Bible study leader meant it to be uplifting, and so often it is, but tonight I feel perforated by guilt.

Thursday 5 October

Woke determined to control tongue until Spouse declined my offer of tea at 6.30 while he pulled on shorts and T-shirt and said, 'I'll have one when I get back from my walk.'

'Do superheroes drink tea?' I said.

So much for resolutions.

Yawned right in Mirror's face this morning. A proper Grand Canyon yawn. Tonsils and all.

'I'm never going to un-see that,' it said.

Why did God give me such wide yawns? Other women yawn discreetly and even elegantly. Me? It takes up the whole of my face. A yawn wearing a haircut.

Finally got round to chlamydia in PHSE. But they're asking questions I can't answer. All I have is a tedious PowerPoint generated by the deputy head with responsibility for Pastoral Care – Colin. Why's he in charge of PHSE anyway? He's near retirement, teaches geography and doesn't look people in the eyes when he talks to them.

Tried Googling 'chlamydia discharge colour' during class discussion to answer one query. Had to minimize the screen fast before they saw the photograph.

Said to Sally later, 'Where on our contracts does it say we'd have to teach about STIs? I trained to educate them about commas, not crabs.'

Drafted email to Colin and suggested the school get experts in. Auntie Google tells me Warwickshire has a school health and well-being service. In an email, gave Colin their phone number, email address, office address and website link. Finished email with, 'I doubt any community nurses ever get asked to teach about the semicolon.' But Sally made me delete it before I pressed Send.

Email pinged ten seconds later, but it was the Head of Year 13. Matt has been 'talked to' about cannabis use, as we can't prove he'd smoked it that morning. Emailed back to say he must have smoked an entire plantation the night before, then.

Camilla has given me an extensive list of things Adrian would like to see in the magazine. Seems he wants a public relations officer, not an editor, and puff-pieces about our Gifted & Talented programme, not thoughtful feature articles or stories by the pupils.

Haven't told Spouse this.

Friday 6 October

Revised homophones with Jim's Year 9. Mini-epiphanies going on all over the room. For some reason, even Year 9s who can spell 'soliloquy' and 'diarrhoea' still write, 'There ball is over their where there playing.'

Year 12 have moved on to discourses, so today we looked at narrative discourse and applied Labov's narrative theory to joke-telling. The Privates started off sceptical, but they enjoyed the lesson. A coup.

It ended awkwardly, though, when a boy said it had been the funnest lesson this term.

'Funnest?' said Gus.

Tense silence. Then the boy said, 'Do you actually want to die young, you posh loser?'

Gus won't try that again. Might pass him a few Bible verses on the power of the tongue.

The Privates have all bought David Crystal books. I am expanding his kingdom and I hope he appreciates it, O blessed be his holy name.

Told Writing Club they were now on my magazine team. Kardashian fan: 'Can I do a piece on butt implants?'

Must check Adrian's list. Sure it'll be on there.

'One more week, and then half-term,' I said to Sally as we packed up at 6 p.m.

She bit her lip. 'I'd check the calendar.'

Oh. Two more weeks.

Pizza Express with Spouse and a couple of friends tonight. Suffered a spate of yawns between main and pudding. Even with both hands, had trouble covering up. 'Are we boring you?' one of our friends said. Then she added, 'Joke!' Which means 'not a joke'.

Monday 9 October

Used first half of double period to set Year 11 a practice question on *Inspector*. Threatened detentions for misdemeanours. 'You need to do your best,' I said, 'and you'll find out why in an hour.'

Suspense pays off. Ian Rankin does pretty well out of it, anyway.

One boy earned a detention within two minutes for disruption. So they were mostly quiet afterwards, scribbling and frowning.

Collected the scripts. 'This is called a blind workshop,' I said. 'Here's how it works. I shuffle your scripts. I choose one at random. I hide the name. I make sure no one can see the writing. I read a paragraph from it. We discuss. We use the mark scheme to grade it. No one knows who wrote it. No one needs to be embarrassed.'

The whole class: 'No!'

Me: 'Trust me.'

When the bell rang for lunch after the blind workshop, I said, 'Who thinks their next literature essay will be better?'

Grudging hands-up from most, including Danny. 'I'd like to own up to that last one you read. The top band paragraph.'

'Sure you would, mate,' said his friend.

Sally was quiet today. She and Archie argued all weekend. He's booked two weeks in the Caribbean for their honeymoon without asking her. 'We can't afford it,' she said to me. 'Money just seems to slip through his hands.'

Year 7 gave in their homework ballads. Marked them tonight. The first was entitled 'A Tradgic Limerick'.

There was once a schoolboy called John
Who's mum said oh where has John gone?
He'd gone to Macdonalds
Whose first name was Ronuld
To get a cheesburger with pickuls on.

Read it to Spouse as he put on his trainers.

'Come with me,' he said, 'and walk off the pain?'

I said, 'Thanks, but I'd need to walk to John o' Groats for that.'

Tuesday 10 October

Ooh, brave. The Head of Science asked Adrian in briefing about the Mocksted rumour. He'd heard that the Chief Inspector of Ofsted had warned against schools carrying out Mocksteds.

I felt Camilla, next to me, stiffen up as though she'd stopped breathing. She's a big fan of Adrian. She even reads the 'Headmaster's Weekly Blog' that everyone else pretends isn't happening. I'm sure his secretary writes it, anyway.

'Staff will be informed of any developments,' Adrian said, after a pause.

Thought Camilla had breathed her last. But then she let a lungful out and was back with us.

Ah well.

Year 7 chorused, 'Have you marked our ballads?' as I arrived. 'Can we all read them out?'

'I've chosen five that I think are the best examples of actual *ballads*,' I said, 'using the conventions I *tried* to teach you.'

Widespread despair, except for the five balladeers, who peacocked it up to the front.

Said to colleagues while Camilla shuffled papers before the lunch-time meeting, 'Where does that enthusiasm go? Even the dyslexics and the stumblers will read out their work in Year 7. By Year 9, they'd rather be garrotted.'

'It gradually leaks out of them,' Sally said.

'Like a tap needing a new washer,' said Jim.

'Like a hose with a hole in it,' Bahlul said.

'Like a cucumber left at the back of the fridge for months,' I said.

They all said, 'Ugh!'

Camilla killed the banter by giving us each a document entitled 'Pedagogical Essentials'.

Later, she came to my Year 13 coursework lesson ostensibly to return their homework essays, but I spied her peering at their computer screens. 'Coursework going well?' she asked Matt.

'What coursework?' he said. 'Miss hasn't, like, told us about any coursework.'

'Matt!' I said.

'But –' Camilla said, glancing at me.

'Joke!' Matt said. 'Lolz!'

Camilla made a little strangled sound.

Spouse had a headache tonight. 'I'll give the power walk a miss,' he said. Felt so much better about myself and was really nice to him all evening.

Wednesday 11 October

Spent my free period prepping next few chapters of *Handmaid* in an empty geography classroom, where no one would look and where Bahlul couldn't talk to me. Just as well – chapter 16's sex scene with the Handmaid and the Commander is full on, and at one point I said 'No!' out loud. Explaining that to Bahlul would have been awkward.

Explaining it to Year 13 in their double period later required my best literary-criticism poker face. Fortunately, most were more embarrassed than I was, especially when Conor asked what 'copulating' meant and Rebekah, strangely the least embarrassed, explained in detail.

Epic fail moment today. In the corridor at lunchtime, saw a sixth-former reading a sheet of paper. As I passed, she looked up. 'Miss, can I ask a question?'

I stopped. It's nice to feel wanted.

She said, 'What does "incomprehensible" mean?'

Came over all keen English teacher and explained that it meant something that couldn't be understood, something unintelligible, confusing, unclear, baffling, mystifying – perhaps, er, bizarre. I ran out of synonyms. 'Why?' I said.

She looked down at the paper. 'Because my history teacher has written it in red capitals at the end of my essay.' She pointed.

All I could manage was, 'Ah, yes. They're quite big capitals.'

Skipped Bible study to mark. Wrote ticks and comments with one eye on a TV drama for half an hour. Then stopped marking and watched with two eyes.

I'm an English teacher. I'm *meant* to study narratives.

Thursday 12 October

Plucked out an inch-long stiff grey hair from my left eyebrow. It stuck out at right angles from my face.

'How did you not see that yesterday?' I said to Mirror. 'I went round all day looking like a hag.'

'Only yesterday?' Mirror said.

Rude.

Not a word from PHSE Colin in reply to my email about getting in experts. Saw him in a corridor and am sure he ducked into the humanities book cupboard. So, Lesson 3 about STIs was all down to me and my poker face, while they asked questions that would make a pimp blush.

Email from Camilla to everyone in department announcing a Key Stage 3 work audit. 'Please select work from each class in Years 7–9,' it said. 'Submit by next Wednesday for the senior management team to examine.'

Fine. But adding 'without fail' won't endear her to anyone.

Bahlul said he'd planned a weekend away. 'But not any more,' he said, doleful. He hasn't marked his Key Stage 3 books since mid-September.

Researched some of Year 11's STI questions at home this evening. My internet history now looks very suspicious, so I hope no one's hacking me.

Friday 13 October

I thought I'd started sleeping better, but last night was the worst for ages. Dragged myself downstairs at 3 to mark Year 11 essays.

This morning, yawned into Mirror again and shocked myself. 'I actually looked like that Munch scream painting then.'

'Incorrect,' Mirror said. 'In the painting, she has her hands around her head.'

Sally brought me cake again on break duty. 'Marry me,' I said.

'If you remember, I'm already getting married,' she said. 'You told the whole school.'

Took copies of the school magazine I produced at my previous school to Writing Club. Wanted to show them the possibilities. Opinion pieces. Advice pieces. Reviews. Creative writing. 'Exhibitions' of art or textiles. Staff and student interviews.

It was a mistake. They spent the session flicking through, pointing at photos and saying, 'I know him! He's in prison now!' and, 'Did you teach her, Miss? She works in Poundland.'

Received a text from my foster parents. Could they pop round on Saturday morning to say hello? They're in the area.

Babysat tonight. Took my marking and managed half a set of Year 8 books. Startled awake by Son and DIL's homecoming at 10.30.

'Any noise from upstairs?' DIL said.

'Not a squeak,' I replied.

Felt guilty. Could have slept through distressed calls of, 'Grandma! A man in a stripy T-shirt and a balaclava is climbing through my window!'

Monday 16 October

Weekend dominated by half-term grade inputting, apart from Saturday visit of FosterMum and FosterDad. They arrived windswept. Hurricane Ophelia bustled up and down our cul-de-sac all day.

Invited Son, DIL and Littluns round too. My foster parents enjoyed grassing me up to everyone with stories about me at fourteen, when I'd tumbled into their family bringing baggage. Not merely the suitcase kind.

'See. You're laughing,' I said. 'I couldn't have been that bad.'

'We're laughing *now*,' my foster mother said.

Bahlul looked strained today as he struggled through the office door with all the marking he'd taken home. 'How do you all do it in so much detail?' he said.

Jim didn't hold back. 'We do it every day. Not every month.'

Gave Camilla my work audit books. She looked disappointed that they were early.

A Monster Calls lesson with Year 8 in Period 2. Someone had written on the whiteboard in green board pen, 'Spoiler! He let's his mother fall of a cliff.'

I thought I wouldn't find the culprit. But when Leon on the front row took his blazer off, a green board pen fell from his pocket.

Kept him back at break. 'Did you flick to the end?' I said.

He looked offended. 'No. I read the whole book. I was just having a laugh. Sorry, Miss.'

Made him practise apostrophes and off/of.

Year 11 group work today, making revision cards. Interrupted by invasion of three wasps, which came one by one as if they'd planned it. As we ejected one, a compatriot arrived.

'They won't kill you!' I said, irritated by the class's fuss and panic.

Just in case, checked SIMS. No, no wasp allergies.

Tuesday 17 October

Not a word about Mocksted in briefing. The Head of Science stayed quiet.

'Do you think he's been hauled in?' Sally said later in the office. 'Had his toenails pulled off?'

'Or given a bottom-set chemistry group,' Jim said.

Taught Year 8 about review writing by showing them reviews of *A Monster Calls*. 'This one's about the film version,' I said.

Shocked faces.

'There's a *film*? And you've made us read the whole book?' As though I'd made them walk over hot coals or chew live insects.

Camilla had almost finished her Top Tips #4 today when she rushed out of the office without warning. Sally followed her, but came back from a futile search. I answered the office phone five minutes later and it was Colin asking if Jim could cover Camilla's Period 5 lesson. She'd gone home ill.

'No problem,' Jim said.

Year 11 parents had been invited in at 7 p.m. for a lecture from the Head of Year about revision. Compulsory attendance for all Year 11 teachers. We got a dry ham baguette and a soapy apple after school as a reward.

Jim volunteered to deliver Camilla's planned English revision talk, using her PowerPoint. Did a great job.

I wish I was as nice as Jim.

I mean, he's an atheist and everything.

Wednesday 18 October

Camilla's not back until after half-term. She sent me work to pass to Years 12 and 13. Sally's sorting her other classes.

'Anyone know what's wrong?' Jim asked at break. We were eating cupcakes provided by the Smuts to thank us for last night. Resented the soapy apple a bit less.

We shook our heads.

'I'll have her cupcake, anyway,' he said. 'What the eye doesn't see.'

Felt reassured.

Political discourses lesson with Year 12, analysing a Theresa May speech and a clip from *Any Questions*. Wish I hadn't. All three Privates are studying politics and had plenty to say. Most of the others gaped at them as though trying to understand fast Mandarin. I sent the Privates to the library for further study and gave us all a break from inferiority.

This week's section of *Handmaid* for Year 13 involved a paragraph about hardcore porn movies and what they depicted.

Might switch to primary school teaching, reading *Biff, Chip & Kipper* with innocent five-year-olds like Grandboy. No hardcore stuff there, unless you're Freud, who'd find plenty.

Bible study tonight in Jean's lounge – all sea-green sofas and tiny bunches of flowers in vases. Bible commentaries and Christian books on the shelves. Was wondering what they'd all think if I said, *Hey, guess what I was teaching today. Let me read you an extract.*

Mind you, that Bible story about Lot's daughters getting him drunk and then one of them 'lying with him' isn't exactly *Biff, Chip & Kipper* either.

Thursday 19 October

In assembly, Year 11 received the same talk as their parents did on Tuesday. Jim stepped in again for Camilla.

Later, after an awkward question and answer session in PHSE, including comment on the #metoo campaign they've all heard about, one girl spoke up. 'That revision lecture. We've heard it twice now. Our parents came home on Tuesday and spouted it word for word.'

'Mine didn't,' a boy called out. 'I haven't even heard it once.'

'But you were in assembly,' I said.

'Had my earphones in, Miss. Too late now to punish. You didn't see me.'

Cordially invited him to my detention at break. 'I'll get you a copy of the PowerPoint,' I said. 'I'd hate you to lose out.'

The cover administrator asked me to take a Year 9 class for Camilla in my free period. Camilla's teaching them *Of Mice and Men*. They're on chapter 2. I idly flicked through one boy's copy while the class was working. Someone had written on the first page, 'BTW, at the end, George shoots Lennie in the head.'

'Did you write this?' I said to the boy.

He looked genuinely upset. 'It's not true, is it, Miss?' He turned to the rest of the class and said loudly, 'Is it true? George shoots Lennie in the head?'

Camilla will hit the roof.

This evening, Spouse told me he's lost three pounds in weight, so I cooked steak and chips and piled up his plate.

Friday 20 October

Last day before the half-term holiday. And a non-uniform day.

But – had a sore throat this morning and felt sniffly. 'You look grim,' said Mirror. 'Happy holidays.'

'I'm going to Cornwall tomorrow, cold or no cold,' I said. 'And you won't be able to come, ha ha.'

'I think you'll find I have relatives in your holiday cottage,' Mirror said.

Jim's Year 9s were yampy. I had forgotten my seating plan and when they're in their own clothes I can't remember all the names. Not my best class control moment.

Felt miserable on break duty.

'At least I don't have to nag passing kids about uniform,' I said to Sally when she brought cake. Spoke too soon. Pulled a Year 9 girl aside to ask where her trousers were. She thought a long T-shirt and fishnet tights constituted an outfit. Sally took her to Lost Property to make her acceptable.

Saw the girl five minutes later in trousers so big and baggy she could have sailed a yacht. She actually scowled.

Cancelled Writing Club. Put a note on the door saying, 'Miss has the plague. See you after half-term.' Must start the magazine soon, though. Time and tide.

'Can we do something fun?' Year 8 said in Period 5.

'My lessons are always –'

They asked me not to give them that old line.

Found YouTube videos featuring children's authors. Distributed giant Post-its. 'As you watch, write ten tips you learn about being a good writer on your Post-it.'

'You're not going to make us *write*.'

'It's a Post-it note.'

'It's still writing.'

'OK. Five tips.'

'Four?'

Didn't have the energy. And Lynne was off sick, so no back-up. Once this class unravelled, I'd never ravel them back.

'Four, and that's the end of it.'

Won't offer myself to the government to help with any trade negotiations.

Second half of autumn term

Monday 30 October

Mirror said this morning, 'No spots. Well done!'

'Don't patronize me. Look at my nose.'

'You've had a cold. That's all.'

'The skin on my nose is peeling away. I have raw flesh underneath. How do I face the world?'

Mirror said I should think of it as new, not raw.

Met Sally walking into school. She asked how Cornwall went.

'Don't look at my peeling nose,' I said.

'It was really enjoyable, thanks, Sally,' she said. 'How was your holiday?'

'Sorry.' I told her it had been lovely to have a sea view while marking, planning, working on the school magazine and sneezing.

'You didn't work all week?'

'In the mornings,' I said, 'while Spouse power walked the entire south coast. Don't tell me you got away with not working.'

She said she'd sweetened the pill by marking in a café. 'Totted up twenty-two hours overall in Warwick Costa. Bankrupted us with my coffee and cake bill.'

'Where was Archie?'

'Away,' she said, but didn't look keen to say more.

I asked if she'd read any good books.

'I wish. Did you?'

'A fabulous Susan Hill book called *Black Sheep*,' I said. 'Bleak and Gothic. Set in a mining village. It doesn't end well.'

She said it didn't sound like a Richard and Judy pick.

'And it was short,' I said. 'A novella. No one took too long to die.'

Camilla brought in a box of chocolates to thank the department for covering for her before the holiday. She also sent us an email. Our Key Stage 3 work audit had 'revealed significant disparity in assessment quality' and 'instant improvement is mandatory'.

No one looked at Bahlul.

In Period 2, a Year 8 boy thought I'd announced that the next new unit of work was on warp poetry. Said he'd liked the sound of it, but then I'd mentioned soldiers.

Double Year 11 working on English Language Paper 1. 'Remember you have mock exams coming up,' I said.

Some denied all knowledge of mock exams. No one had mentioned them – they were certain.

'But surely the holiday revision I set would have reminded you.'

Floor and ceiling suddenly fascinating.

Tuesday 31 October

Shock revelation in briefing. Adrian has shaved his head. None of us knew where to look, as though he'd taken his trousers off. Presumably given up on comb-overing. Granted, it has been breezy lately.

Rumours about Mocksted still bounce around the corridors, but Adrian said nothing.

Email from Colin. Thanked me for PHSE suggestion and 'detailed information', but budget constraints won't allow for expert visits. He is sure I will deliver this half-term's materials on healthy eating with wisdom and skill.

Showed Sally the email at break while we necked as many of Camilla's chocolates as we could and drank tepid coffee from the staffroom machine.

'Budget constraints?' Sally said. 'What about Mocksted?'

Camilla wants to meet me on Wednesday to discuss the magazine. 'Anything in particular?' I asked. But she wasn't telling.

Year 7 seem happy about reading Roald Dahl's *Boy* this half-term. I displayed the word 'autobiographical' and challenged them to find words of three or more letters in it. Who knew that the word 'bog' could produce so much entertainment so many, many times over?

This evening, Spouse informed me he has been reading up on Christian mindfulness and joined a website that delivers half-hour meditations.

'What brought that on?' I asked.

He said I made it sound like a stomach bug. 'I knew it wouldn't be your thing. But one of my clients mentioned it. He says it centres him.'

'Centres? Why do you need centring? In what way are you off-kilter?'

'I'm not. But the client said it helped him after his wife died.'

'Oh.'

'And I know Mum hasn't gone yet, but –'

'Where will you do it? In the lounge? With candles?'

'In the lounge if you're upstairs marking in the study, I suppose. Or I'll use the spare bedroom.'

Seriously. I'm not sure I know who Spouse is any more. He's always been more keen on peace and silence and watching bees than I am. But it's a bit New Agey, isn't it?

If he starts chanting, what do I do?

Wednesday 1 November

Had meeting with Camilla. Adrian is enriching my Writing Club with three Pupil Premium Year 10s to make sure we're offering 'stretch' opportunities to deprived pupils. She showed me their names: Charlotte, Bella, Lukas.

'I don't know them,' I said. 'I don't teach Year 10 and none of them were in my Year 9s last year. Do they like writing? Will they want to help with the magazine? Do they *want* to come?'

'Don't shoot the messenger,' she said.

It's a good thing I wasn't holding the staple gun.

Started language change with Year 12. Challenged them to think of twenty contemporary words I wouldn't have known when I was sixteen. 'Telephone' was one offering.

So many homework-shirkers today. Chasing them is tiring, like when the wind blows away your bus ticket and whips it this way and that while you snatch at it.

Year 13 sat a practice question on *Handmaid*. Four wrote less than half a page, then stopped. What else to do then but stare at your teacher, sitting at the desk marking books? Felt like a museum exhibit. At least my nose no longer resembles raw meat. Thank you, Vaseline. But I did treat Year 13 to a few uber-yawns.

Jim said later, 'I sit on the back row during tests. Spy on *them* instead. It puts the wind up the ne'er-do-wells.'

Jim has the best ideas.

At Bible study, Spouse told the others about the Christian mindfulness. Two took the website details. He's starting a cult!

Thursday 2 November

Another Year 11 assembly on revision, only this time Marion Coles delivered it. She could be forty, could be fifty. Recently divorced, Sally told me. But so funny. Jo Brand, but with a Texan drawl.

'Some of you know me as a history teacher, but I'm also deputy head of teaching and learning here at Beauchamp,' she began.

Year 11 shifted in their seats.

'I guess that makes me sound like a boring old fart,' she went on.

They sat up a bit. Teachers don't say 'fart' in assemblies.

Marion spoke, without crib sheets, about motivation, organization, timetabling and study methods – subjects Adrian or Colin would have reduced to the educational equivalent of All Bran.

I noticed Jim laughing at her jokes.

In my PHSE lesson afterwards, Year 11 were predictably complimentary about Mrs Coles. They wish she was their history teacher. They think she's a legend. They want to know why all teachers can't be like her.

Took my revenge by PowerPointing them to death with Colin's fascinating facts about vitamins.

Off timetable from mid-morning, my lessons covered by other teachers. Educational theatre company in the hall, helping Year 11 to understand *An Inspector Calls*. Pam organized it before she went off sick and it took her weeks to persuade Adrian it was worth funding.

Half the theatre company were ex-teachers. Sally said to me as they left, 'Off home now, they are. No marking. Maybe learning some lines. Reading a play.'

'Don't.' I put my hand on my chest. 'It hurts my heart.'

A group of my Year 7s spotted me at home time. 'You were *in school*?' they cried, as though I'd deliberately hidden from them and wasn't at home with severe diarrhoea and vomiting as was only right and fair.

Asked Jim why he'd been in the Year 11 assembly. 'You don't have a Year 11 form.'

'Just interested,' he said.

Friday 3 November

Can't decide whether I'd rather have two chin spots very close together, as today, or two far apart on different areas of my face. People have the same debate over whether to have twins and get it all over with, or two children with a decent gap in between.

Had another look at Adrian's list of desirable features for the magazine. Compared it with my list.

Perhaps he'll forget he ever compiled his.

'We didn't like the cover teacher on Friday,' Year 7 complained. 'He made us read in silence and threatened detentions if we talked.'

'That's probably because I wrote "Make them read in silence, and threaten detentions if they talk" on the instructions,' I said.

You'd think I'd sold them to a slave trader.

Writing Club farcical. Told the usual crew that three new members were coming. The fuss! 'Look, we're not the Freemasons,' I said.

Uh?

Tied myself in knots explaining Freemasonry badly.

While we waited for the new arrivals, informed the group that I'd made a unilateral democratic decision to call the magazine *Beauchamp Matters*.

No new pupils came. Saw Camilla passing computer room. Raced out to ask if she knew why. By the time she'd rounded them up, we had five minutes left – enough time to work out that Lukas looks like a Greek god. James, a clever, gaunt boy pushing six feet already, looked forlorn at Lukas's arrival. Beside each other, they look like chalk and everything else not chalk.

Good news, though. The no-show wasn't deliberate. No one had told them when and where. They seem quite keen, in fact.

Does anyone say 'forlorn' now? Miranda Hart would say it to camera: 'For-lorn. What an interesting word! Foooor-loooorrn.'

Monday 6 November

Son and DIL visited friends at the weekend, so Grandboy and Grandgirl came for Saturday sleepover. Took them to Leamington for tea.

Since when did a kid's two scoops of vanilla and a half-flake dessert change to three scoops of different flavours, bedecked with Maltesers, mini-marshmallows, chocolate sprinkles, popping candy and a neon-pink sauce you could run the National Grid with? Prayed they wouldn't be sick in the night.

They weren't. But they weren't sleepy either, having mainlined toxic chemicals.

At 9.30 p.m. they finally settled. 'You can't start marking now, on a Saturday evening,' Spouse said, as I fished a sheaf of essays from my rucksack.

'Watch me.'

Grandgirl was sleeping in the study and Grandboy in the spare room, so I had to mark at the dining table. Spouse plugged in earphones to listen to something downloaded to his tablet. He kept saying 'Pah' so I think it was a Radio 4 politics programme, not a meditation.

Twin spots still throbbing away this morning. Tried shouting, 'Out, damned spots!' It worked for me as well as it worked for Lady Macbeth.

Mirror said, 'Let's hope that's the end of the similarities between her destiny and yours.'

Had run short of concealer and might have had to use peanut butter. But bought new tube at the weekend. Am convinced the teenage sales assistant was staring at my face, agog at how much needed concealing.

May buy online in future.

Year 11 wrote a story in their double lesson today, inspired by a picture of a fireworks display. 'Isn't that weird?' one girl said. 'It was Guy Fawkes Day yesterday! And today we get this picture in English!'

'Dur,' said the girl sitting beside her. 'Miss planned it like that.'

The first girl gazed at me. 'Miss, that is so lovely of you to take the time.' As though she thought I spent my evenings on a couch being fed grapes.

'Just call me SuperTeach.' I flicked my cardigan back as though it were a cloak, but I swept a pen from the desk and had to fish it from the bin.

What if 'Pah' *is* one of the chants?

Tuesday 7 November

It's happening. We're being Mocksteded on Tuesday 5 December. Adrian announced it in briefing, running his hand backwards and forwards across his now-bald pate as though, if he smoothed that, he could quell mutiny.

By the time the department meeting started at lunchtime, we'd all received a clutch of fat emails with ominous headings such as 'Mocksted Essentials' and 'Mocksted Preparation Checklist'.

Camilla was about to speak when Jim said, 'Do you think companies who sell manure get inspected by Mucksted?'

Then Bahlul said companies that sold raincoats would get 'Macsted'.

Camilla had to interrupt our giggling with, 'Have we quite finished?'

'It's nervous tension, Camilla,' Jim said. 'My granddad told me how before they left the trenches to go over the top, they cracked jokes to calm their fears.'

She was unmoved.

Her Top Tips #5 session was all about making our classrooms into 'positive learning spaces'. The Smuts want displays to be 'dynamic' and 'an interactive pedagogical resource'.

Translation: spend two hours after school every fortnight replacing old work.

Hope she hasn't checked Bahlul's classroom. There's work on his boards from pupils who've graduated from uni, married and had three children. He may well have those children in his classes now.

Wednesday 8 November

Twin spots fading at last. Now for the under-eye bags. Saw an advert in a magazine yesterday for a white concealer made by a glamorous cosmetics company. It makes you look 'super-awake' and 'radiant'.

Mirror said, 'A bag over your head would be cheaper.'

The company carrying out our Mucksted is called 'Resolutions Educational Consultants'.

'Again, how can the school afford this?' Sally asked me and Jim in the office.

Jim predicted that the flapjacks next year would be one centimetre squared. He said his friend's a headteacher whose school was Mucksteded. 'She says it sucked all the life out of them getting it perfect for Mucksted, so that when Ofsted turned up only a week later, no one could be bothered, and they went into special measures.'

Year 12 and Year 13 classes both slashed by an art trip. Camilla said this morning, 'Make sure you chase the artists to catch up on the work they've missed.'

'I think school policy is that they come to us,' I said.

Her eyes widened but she hardly missed a beat. 'Please circulate the work to their form tutors without delay.'

Her eyes are an unusual colour – a kind of green. And the pupils are tiny.

Missed Bible study again. Marked until 9.30 p.m., but then one essay blurred into another, so poured a Baileys. Was watching telly with a glass in my hand when Spouse came back at 9.40 to say he'd shared with the group how hard I was working and they'd all prayed fervently for me.

Thursday 9 November

Woke at 3 last night, sure I had palpitations. Went downstairs to ask Auntie Google for reasons. There are many, among them late-evening alcohol and stress.

Chose stress.

In PHSE Healthy Eating #2, Year 11 calculated how many teaspoons of sugar they eat in an average day's meals and drinks. The winner, with fifty-two teaspoons consumed yesterday, was a girl who plays tennis, hockey and netball, and looks like a supermodel. She drinks at least three cans of Monster a day.

The others gasped.

'Those energy drinks have twelve teaspoons of sugar each,' I said. 'And the equivalent of four shots of coffee.'

Her circulatory system must be half caramel cappucino! I kept her back after the lesson to say I was concerned. She told me that her mum and dad are proud of her sporting achievements. She doesn't want to let them down. She spends most evenings and every weekend training or playing. The drinks get her through. Her parents keep a stock in the fridge.

'The drinks don't seem to help with my homework,' she said. 'It's always rubbish.'

'Don't you get palpitations from all the caffeine?' I asked.

She said she didn't know the word.

I said, 'A fluttery heart?'

Her hand went to her sternum and her blazer sleeve fell back. I saw tiny scars on her forearm.

Studied Wilfred Owen's poem 'Disabled' with Year 8, comparing it with 'Dulce et Decorum est'. One boy said he'd wanted to join the army like his dad and grandad, but the war poems had changed his mind.

'Because of the suffering?' I said.

No, not that. He didn't want to risk meeting boring people who wrote poems. I could see Lynne at the back trying not to laugh.

Sally showed me her phone after school. 'Have you seen this? All Delhi schools are closed for a *week* because of smog. Imagine!'

'That's terrible.'

'No! I mean, imagine being a Delhi teacher. A whole week off! What I'd give for a week off right now.'

'For wedding plans?' I said.

A non-committal 'Hm'.

Told Sally about the Monster girl. 'Submit a Child Protection form,' she said.

'I thought so,' I said.

I rang the Head of Year 11, who said, 'You will have met her parents last year. Enormous people. They must both be morbidly obese.'

'Ah yes,' I said. 'I remember now.'

Home at 7. Spouse was in the lounge with his eyes closed and the lights off. A deep, melodious voice was reciting a psalm until Spouse switched it off, blinking, when he noticed me.

Felt as though I'd made a clumsy entrance wearing heavy boots into a quiet country church.

Friday 10 November

Year 7 were shocked at the chapter in *Boy* when the boys get viciously caned by the headmaster. Dahl doesn't hold back. 'What year was this?' someone asked, and the rest nodded.

'The 1920s,' I said.

General sigh of relief. Ancient history.

'But,' I said, 'caning was only finally abolished in all British schools in 1998. Just nineteen years ago.'

'What?'

Have set them weekend homework to ask grandparents and parents if they'd been caned at school. Lynne said Monday's lesson should be interesting.

In Writing Club, we tussled with a list of magazine sections. Would have been anarchy if I hadn't already prepared. Our Kardashian expert made the most fuss. But we finally agreed on four: Pupil Experience, Culture and Creativity, School Events, and Staff and Pupil Profiles. I divided them into work teams, playing to their interests, and gave them jobs to do for next week.

'Homework?' they said. 'But –'

'Look,' I said. 'Tell me now if you don't think you can commit. It's going to be hard work.'

Kardashian-girl said, baldly, 'I don't wanna commit.'

One down. Seven left.

Lukas wants to write about sports events within school, especially athletics. James offered to review science-fiction novels for the Culture section.

Raced to Pizza Express after work to meet family at 6. Wine. Antipasti. Littluns in their free chef hats, saying 'Urrgggh' when trying olives. If only there'd been no rucksack by my chair, straining at its seams and getting in the waiter's way.

Monday 13 November

Talked to lady from Bible study group during after-church coffee yesterday. She has white hair like God. I think she is 129 and has been spared death because she's doing so well. She told me she takes every opportunity to share her faith.

'We're not supposed to proselytize at school,' I said, 'so I can't mention it in class.' Tried to look professional and policy-abiding.

'Not at all?' she said. 'You can't even say that you attend church?'

Fortunately, someone then spilled hot coffee into their lap and there was a hubbub.

Spouse brought a toasted sandwich up to the study at 9 last night. I was five exercise books from victory. 'Finish those tomorrow,' he said. 'You've been marking all weekend. If you were part-time, you'd be watching telly now.'

'That's not helpful. Year 11 mocks start tomorrow.' Sixty exam papers on the horizon. Like an approaching meteorite.

The preacher's sermon yesterday was interesting. All about perspective. Things don't have to drag you down – try a different angle.

This morning I approached Mirror sideways on.

Got carried away with magazine planning in Period 1 and didn't hear the bell. The office phone rang at 10.15. It was Camilla to tell me she was outside my classroom, where my Year 8s were impersonating a wild-bear enclosure. Did I intend to teach them today?

When I arrived, she tutted with her whole body.

Year 11 are doing exams in the hall, so no double lesson with them today. Answered emails, planned lessons and rang round local printing companies, finding out prices.

How much?

Year 7 lesson entirely taken up playing Harrowing Corporal Punishment Stories Top Trumps.

Tuesday 14 November

Briefing was all Mucksted and no time for notices, so my planned announcement about the magazine and call for support will have to wait. Sent Adrian a list of the printing companies' prices afterwards.

More corporal punishment stories from Year 7. Canes. Belts. Paddles. Board rubbers. 'Are you feeling grateful?' I said.

One had misunderstood. He had a great-great-great-great granddad who'd been hanged for murder.

Explained difference between corporal and capital. Again.

Year 12 studying how grammar changes over time. Discussed grammatical misunderstandings. Some shocked to find that 'could of' isn't a thing. The Privates were shocked to find other Year 12s who thought it *was* a thing.

English department meeting was all about preparations for Mucksted. Jim called it Mucksted throughout the meeting. But Camilla can't tell him off – he was a saint when she was away, even doing her marking.

St Jim the Atheist. It has a ring to it.

Year 13 reluctant to hand over their coursework drafts. (Not you, Rebekah.) This does not bode well.

Rebekah must be a Christian. She said 'Praise the Lord' when I told her I thought her coursework was already top band. I checked her face to see if it was ironic, but I don't think so.

53

Spouse has lost four pounds now, whereas I've put on weight since September. 'If you're wondering where you lost your pounds,' I told him, 'they're round my waist.'

Wednesday 15 November

The office is awash with Year 11 scripts from yesterday's mock. Everyone's desk bears a pile, secured in an elastic band. Two essays per paper: 1. *An Inspector Calls*. 2. Paper 1 English Language.

The usual chaos. Anyone with Special Educational Needs did their paper in a different room, and those papers are still snailing their way back to the department. I have three missing. Also, Bahlul and I have a pupil with a similar name and received each other's scripts.

Surprise! Adrian emailed to say go for the cheapest printer for the magazine. That means, presumably, he can now order in the Mucksted consultants' lunches from Fortnum & Mason.

Year 12 unhappy. I ambushed them with nineteenth-century complex sentences and they struggled to their feet when the bell rang, defeated. Even Gus Private looked ashen.

Kept some pupils behind for a lecture about late homework. The broken-printer excuse wears thin. 'There are printers in school,' I reminded them, 'in the library.'

'The library?' one said, as though I'd directed them to the frozen wastes of the Antarctic.

In Year 13 lesson, looked up Jezebel's story in the Bible. 'It'll help explain chapter 36 for you,' I said, 'when the Commander takes the Handmaid to the men's club called Jezebel's.' But when we reached the part in the Bible where Jezebel is thrown out of a window and eaten by stray dogs until only her skull, feet and palms of her hands are left, Conor said, 'I thought the Bible was all about shepherds and fishermen and people getting miracled.'

Rebekah said, 'Try reading it. And anyway, "miracled" isn't a word.'

'Don't tell us you've read the whole thing,' Conor said.

'Four times,' she said spikily, 'for your information.'

She's a Christian all right. But maybe not a natural evangelist.

Started marking exam papers in Period 5, but Bahlul was there, so moved to library. Recovered from a giant yawn during which my whole face shut down, opening my eyes to see Camilla. She was waiting to talk about punctuality to lessons and why spoiling *Of Mice and Men* for an entire class is unwise.

I'd rather only the dentist saw that much of my oral cavity.

Nearly fell asleep in Bible study. Jean's lounge was warm and we were discussing a hefty theoretical passage from the book of Romans. I know it's good for me to learn more about the Bible, but I won't lie. Tonight I hankered after a bit of Jezebel.

Thursday 16 November

Woke at 4. Spouse found me marking Year 11 papers downstairs at 6.30. He made me tea. Didn't tell him I'd already had three cups.

Year 11 assembly cancelled because the hall is set up for mock exams. Saw George in there, replacing some desks. He said a dad had complained that his daughter was sitting her mocks at a desk bearing a message carved with a compass: 'No good at maths? Snort crack instead.' Caretakers had been asked to check each desk for any further unacceptable etchings.

No PHSE. Marked scripts in the far corner of a science lab.

Might have known it was too good to be true. Was hunted down and asked to cover Year 8 maths lesson in Period 2. 'I teach English only,' I told the class, 'for good reason. So, if you had to ask three people in the room to help you with maths,' I said, 'who would they be?'

Three coy candidates were singled out.

'You are duly elected maths consultants,' I said, 'should anyone get stuck. You get a merit for agreeing.'

They agreed.

Zak in Year 7 still causing trouble to Angel Child. 'He won't shut up, Miss. And his language is vile.'

'I'll have to move you again, Zak,' I said.

But Angel Child sighed and said, 'It's OK, Miss. I can deal with it. My little brother is just as annoying.'

I think she likes Zak, despite everything. He is a handsome boy, with his dark hair and bright blue eyes.

Gave him another warning.

Friday 17 November

Period 1 with Year 7 – Roald Dahl's chapter about having his adenoids out without anaesthetic in 1924 isn't quite as disturbing as the caning chapter, but they were horrified.

They wanted to ask relatives for gruesome medical stories. I refused, saying I wasn't spending next Monday's lesson hearing about people writhing while having their haemorrhoids done.

Wished I'd picked hernias as an example instead.

Have renamed the Senior Writing Club 'Journos'. They like this. They're miffed, though. They approached teachers to support the magazine and hardly any knew we were producing one. They'd been rebuffed unceremoniously by some.

Explained that the announcement had got postponed. 'I'll try again Tuesday and back up with an AllStaff email,' I promised.

We focused on opinion and advice writing today. Asked them to think about suitable topics for the Pupil Experience section and bring ideas next week.

The Pupil Premium Three have integrated like butter. I'd expected trouble. Am ashamed of my preconceptions.

Missed a friend's birthday until I saw it on Facebook and seventeen others had sent comments. Worse, posted my favourite happy birthday grumpy-cat-with-a-party-blower GIF on her timeline only to realize someone else already had.

More bad news: a rejection from *TES* for an article idea I'd pitched. Won't tell the Journos. Need my credibility.

Rejections sting. Especially without anaesthetic.

Baileys! Writers' morphine!

Monday 20 November

A cold weekend. After a morning's marking on Saturday, went with Spouse to meet Son and DIL in the park to watch the Littluns hurtle around getting toasty while we shivered and our lips went blue.

DIL asked why I didn't wear a hat. Looked around. Several grandmas in the park were sporting olive green or beige felt hats. Have I got to that stage? Rummaging around charity shops for hats cleared out of dead old ladies' wardrobes?

Led worship yesterday. Didn't have much time to prepare, so fumbled a few chords and confused the other musicians. Someone commented after church, 'I didn't like that second song.' They didn't intend to be mean, I'm sure, but it nagged.

Got four hours' sleep.

'Look at these dark shadows under my eyes,' I said to Mirror this morning. I dabbed on white cream. The packaging had promised much. 'I'm doing this wrong. I look like an extra on the "Thriller" video. Look!'

'I'm looking,' Mirror said. 'It's not as if I have a choice.'

Year 8 were meant to write an essay in silence, comparing two war poems. Cue ten minutes of interruptions. (No pen. No book. No poems. No ideas. No bladder control.) Wrote on board in giant letters, 'Dictionary definition of silence: complete absence of sound.' It worked. Sort of.

Year 11 back from mocks. In a week, they're doing speaking and listening assessments.

'In front of a *camera*? A *speech*?' they said. 'With everyone in the class *watching*?'

'You already know this,' I said. 'You've been preparing for weeks.'
No response.

'You *should* have been preparing for weeks.'

Sixth-form open evening, so arrived home at 8 to cold pizza. Had forgotten to tell Spouse I'd be late.

At 9 p.m. I'm in bed writing this. I should be marking Year 11 exams. They were belly-aching about their grades today.

Am having Baileys with my guilt.

Tuesday 21 November

Snatched my chance in briefing to announce *Beauchamp Matters*. Told colleagues that pupils would produce the material, but begged for staff support: encouragement, guidance, collecting submissions, maybe a little proofreading . . .

Adrian cut in. 'The magazine will showcase Beauchamp School and all its benefits.'

'And we want some staff profiles,' I said, 'if there are volunteers.'

All eye contact *gone*.

In Year 8 lesson, introduced pupils to an American Civil War poem. Leon wanted to know how one could wage a 'civil' war. 'My mum's always telling me to be civil. How does that work?'

'Good point,' I said. We asked Auntie Google, who told us it was to do with citizens – civilians – being at war, not the politeness meaning. Then I showed them an online etymological dictionary, in case they ever wanted to look up the origins of words, and they wanted to look up the origin of swearwords, so we went back to the poem.

Awkward department meeting. Camilla led a group tour around the English classrooms, pointing out exemplary dynamic interactive pedagogical displays.

Sally 5–Bahlul 0.

Me, probably a 2. Year 7 have typed up their gathered tales of corporal punishment and illustrated them. Some quite graphically.

'Why did they do this work?' Camilla asked.

'Roald Dahl's *Boy*,' I said. 'Maybe I should have pinned up an explanation. Some context.'

'By the end of the day, please.'

Had to scrape together a last-minute lesson on close analysis for Year 13, as I haven't marked their coursework drafts yet.

Sent back-up email to AllStaff about *Beauchamp Matters* to try and convince them that it does.

Wednesday 22 November

Had a restless night.

Spouse arrived in the kitchen where I was eating toast at 4, rubbing his eyes. He said, 'Toast? I thought the house was on fire.'

Finally finished marking Year 13 drafts in my free period and through break. Left a grease mark on Rebekah's, though. Too much butter in the break-time flapjack. Hoped she wouldn't notice.

'Is this butter?' she said, when I distributed the work. 'I'm vegan.'

Assured her that now it was dry it was probably safe.

'Vegan?' Matt said. 'You mean, like, you eat, like, just seeds?'

Rebekah hard-stared him like Medusa hard-stared people, and we all know how that turned out.

'Soooooooo,' I said. 'Let's turn to chapter 39.'

At school until 6 finishing Year 11 scripts (woo-hoo!), then inputting their marks and data into spreadsheets. Spreadsheets weren't a thing when I trained as a medical secretary in the 1970s. But then nor were computers. And electric typewriters were new kids on the block.

I go way back. Said to Year 12 today, 'When I was your age, in the Tudor era . . .' and only the Privates got it without having to think.

Bible study cancelled tonight. Jean and the leader of the group both have flu. Hurrah!

I cooked dinner, listened to the radio and drank wine while Spouse went for energetic power walk followed by a meditation upstairs.

Said to him over pork and bean casserole, 'Why stir yourself up then calm yourself down? Just sit on the sofa and have a beer.'

Power walks. Meditations. It's all so deep and purposeful. Why can't he be shallow like other spouses?

Spouses? Spice? Spousen?

Prayed for the recovery of the flu sufferers at 9 p.m., when the dangers of a miracle healing and the reinstatement of Bible study had passed.

Thursday 23 November

Slept pretty well last night. When Bible study is cancelled, I go to bed less guilty. Even a bar of Fruit & Nut after dinner didn't give me as much guilt as reading about the Good Samaritan does. Am fairly sure this is my fault, not the Good Samaritan's.

Taught about carbs in PHSE. Too many Year 11 girls flinched at the word, as though I'd said 'arsenic'. 'You need them,' I said. 'Who's saying you don't?'

Hm. YouTube has a lot to answer for, it seems. Clean eating. Lean eating. Green eating. And not eating.

Did Adele achieve nothing?

Gave Year 11 class their mock papers back. Should never have said, 'If anyone has questions . . .' while they were reading their marks and comments. They had 793 and today's planned speaking and listening preparation died a death.

Beauchamp Matters posters have gone up, courtesy of the Journos. Inbox now stacked with emails from keen Year 7s and 8s wanting to submit pieces about Justin Bieber, cats, horses, Justin Bieber, cupcakes and Justin Bieber. One of my Year 7s has sent unsolicited a detailed description of his great-grandfather's tooth extraction without anaesthetic. Have prepared a response I can copy and paste: 'Thank you for your submission, but your idea is not quite right for the magazine this time.'

The power.

One superb review of the latest school play by a Year 9 boy called Samuel. Funny and sharp. Shame he's too young for the Journos. I suppose we could co-opt him.

Friday 24 November

Seriously? Another spot, right on the end of my nose?

Mirror said this morning, 'I think you'll find that spot is Fruit & Nut flavoured.'

'Ugh. Please don't do that,' I said.

If only concealer on the end of your nose didn't look as though you'd dipped your head in a bowl of hummus.

Followed up from yesterday's PHSE with my Year 11 form during registration. 'Who's had toast or cereal – or both – this morning?'

Half the group.

The other half: blueberries with fat-free yogurt, crisps, strawberry laces, leftover spring roll, Twix. Or a combination. Or nothing at all.

Played Jim's Year 9 some Radio 4 clips to show how politicians use connectives to prevent people interrupting them. A Conservative minister got seventeen 'ands', thirteen 'becauses' and twenty-five 'buts' past the interviewer. Year 9 had fun role-playing interviews, although one boy put his hand over his interviewee's mouth and held it there, so I had to take him to break duty with me.

Mucksted jitters are taking hold of staff now that it's only ten days away. The Smuts keep popping into lessons pretending to do 'learning walks', but they're really spying. Have told my classes to put their hands up, use long words like 'furthermore' and say, 'This is such challenging work, Miss,' when the Smuts are present.

Journos were on fire. Full of ideas for articles about pupil experiences. Bullying. The disadvantages of mixed-sex PHSE lessons. Homework pressures. Uniform regulations. The shift into GCSEs.

School toilets. Dating schoolfriends. 'You'll need to choose two or three,' I said, 'and some are controversial. Might have to check them out with Mr Parkes.'

'What happened to journalistic autonomy?' James said.

Short silence, then, 'Yeah!' said all the others. Like sheep.

'Definition of "autonomy"?' I said.

Betsy sacrificed herself. 'Er – it's like – stars and stuff. The Milky Way. Isn't it?'

James explained. Still, it gave him one over on Lukas for a few seconds.

Spouse has lost another pound. He is gradually de-paunching himself.

Marked upstairs, aided and abetted by a box of Maltesers. Spouse was being mindful downstairs. Could hear piano music, and it certainly wasn't Elton John.

Monday 27 November

Ate fish and chips on Saturday evening with friends. The other wife said she was on a diet and ordered mini-fish, so I did too.

That's the first time I've seen chips bigger than the fish. Had toast and jam and a bowl of cereal before bed.

Harry and Meghan have announced their engagement. News broke by lunchtime and the pupils, girls particularly, could speak of little else. Took Year 11s into computer room to spruce up their speaking and listening PowerPoints. Kept three girls behind for checking news websites for engagement ring pictures instead.

So, twenty minutes sliced off my lunch. This could turn one into a Republican.

At least four Mucksted emails a day land in our inboxes from Adrian and the two deputies, Marion and Colin, with the words 'urgent' and 'important' used like confetti. They begin to contradict each other now, as to what's happening where and when, so no one knows what's going on. 'Like Cluedo,' Sally said. 'Or one of those murder mystery weekends, only without the wine to make it bearable.'

I might get observed by a faux-inspector. Will need to plan all five of Tuesday's lessons in expectation. And by 'plan' they don't mean three bullet points in my teacher's planner. They mean detailed lesson plans, lists of students, seating plans, copies of resources, copy of scheme of work, swimming certificates and latest utilities bill.

Tuesday 28 November

Killer blow from Camilla. Blow from Killer Camilla. She sashayed into the office this morning saying that she wanted to see all our lesson materials for next Tuesday.

Bahlul, who was next to me, grabbed my hand.

'Couldn't you have given more notice?' Jim said, though he said it gently.

Silence.

'I didn't mean now,' she said. 'Put copies on my desk for tomorrow morning.' And she sashayed out again.

'I bet she did mean now,' Sally said. 'You saved us, Jim.'

Bahlul said that all his materials were in his head and hadn't made it out yet.

'Does she mean seating plans and everything?' Sally asked.

Jim raised his eyebrows.

'Surely this is unreasonable,' I said.

'Happens in some schools all the time,' he said. 'Maybe we're lucky.'

Bahlul didn't look as though he felt lucky.

Year 8 are studying Hardy's poem 'The Man He Killed'. 'What do all the dashes in the poem suggest?' I asked, hoping they'd spotted the speaker's guilty hesitations and pauses.

'No, they *weren't* the f-word!'

Was impressed by Year 11's speaking and listening presentations. Fitted five into the lesson, including, 'Why watch YouTube cats?' (shallow and unplanned, but funny), 'Why become a vegan?' (interesting but unfunny) and 'Is there a slave in your street?' (fluent, meticulously researched and terrifying).

The cats talk scraped a pass. The slave talk got full marks. Each speaker got a clap and a lolly.

More on Thursday.

Lunchtime meeting consisted of Camilla ushering us into our classrooms again and asking (Not you, Sally) why nothing had changed since last week. (Because we don't have lives?) She appointed poor Sally as consultant and produced a boxful of literary posters. We spent half an hour staple gunning and straightening. We removed anything labelled 'My homwork'.

Home at 8 after organizing and writing next Tuesday's lesson materials for Camilla. Like compiling a detailed itinerary when you don't even know where you're going.

Spouse had gone out for a drink with a friend and left a plate of chicken casserole.

Typed up speaking and listening assessments. Watched YouTube cats.

Wednesday 29 November

Sally's birthday. She brought three choices of cake: ginger, carrot and lemon. She's testing out flavours for the wedding. Jim said he'd be happy to be chief tester and try all three. Camilla took a slice so small she expended more calories in lifting it than she gained eating it. I suppose she's satiated herself with the lesson materials for Tuesday with which we all covered her desk.

Good to hear Sally talking about the wedding. She rarely mentions Archie at the moment.

Finished *Handmaid* today. 'Admit it,' I said to Year 13. 'It's a brilliant novel and you're glad you've studied it.'

Conor chanted like a robot, 'It's a brilliant novel and I'm glad I've studied it.'

'It was fab,' Rebekah said. Funny. She's kind of Puritan in demeanour but gobbled up all of Atwood's dystopia and sexual deviance as though they were tomato sandwiches.

Next, we're reading *The Road* by Cormac McCarthy. 'You have to compare it with *Handmaid* in Paper 2,' I told them.

What I didn't say was, *If you thought Atwood was dark . . .*

I've eaten nothing but cake all day, and a bowl of porridge before Bible study, as we were late.

Free periods today were taken up with revising all my Mucksted preparation. Crushed by self-doubt. What Camilla has is Version 1. Am now on Version 4.5. Must remember to update student information in my planner in case someone's recently been diagnosed epileptic, dyslexic, apoplectic or antiseptic.

Will get out of bed and write it on my to-do list, otherwise I'll never get to sleep.

Thursday 30 November

Adrian susurrated his way through a talk about Meghan and Harry in the Year 11 assembly, making tenuous links between the engagement and the pupils taking life's opportunities. Am certain he didn't put the PowerPoint together – it was all lovey-dovey words and fluffy pictures. Probably his secretary, Barbara. She loves the Royals and has only corgi pictures on her desk, despite having four children.

Adrian looked odd in his grey suit and tie, standing next to a giant screen full of floating hearts. He's still shaving his head. Has obviously decided on it as his new look.

Ditched Colin's PHSE PowerPoint this week in favour of some fresh-faced YouTubers talking sense about healthy eating. Made

Year 11 take notes in their books and highlight any facts they hadn't known before.

The girl who drank three Monsters a day stayed behind. 'My parents have taken the heat off since school rang them. I've dropped the hockey.'

'*And* the Monsters?'

She nodded.

Asked her how she was feeling.

'Really different. Clearer. My grades have improved.' She paused. 'School told Mum and Dad about my scars.'

'I couldn't not report it,' I said. 'I'm sorry.'

'It's OK,' she said.

Among today's Year 11 presentations: 'Will there be a Third World War?', 'Transgender teens' and 'Keeping ferrets – why everyone should do it'. All good passes.

They're really making an effort, although the lollies, not the certificate they'll receive next summer, seem to be the main driver.

Year 8 enjoyed drawing and labelling the fat, red-faced complacent major described in Sassoon's vicious poem 'Base Details', although one gave him white hair and a long beard like Santa.

Must re-explain the concept of satire.

Checked the school's list of medical conditions. One new entry: someone in my Year 7 class is allergic to wet wipes and comes out in angry rashes. Grateful for warning. Will cross 'swab them all down' off my Mucksted lesson plans.

Friday 1 December

Found a long eyebrow hair in each eyebrow. 'I hope this won't be a regular occurrence,' I said to Mirror.

'Me too,' it said. 'It gives me no pleasure watching you pluck at yourself like a fowl being prepared for the pot.'

Didn't sleep well. Mucksted dreams, in which I end up teaching geography. I arrive at school at lunchtime. There are parents in my classes. The inspectors are my foster parents. Camilla has her nose pressed to the classroom window.

Spent my free time in Period 4 tidying my desk into piles: marked, to mark, to plan, to photocopy, to distribute, to query, to remind myself why I kept this.

No time to mark.

The Journos devised a list of possible titles for opinion/advice pieces, which I've sent to Adrian:

'Homework – does it ruin family evenings?'
'Choosing GCSEs – dos and don'ts'
'Bullying – why so cruel at school?'
'The dating game – when your boyf sits next to you in maths'
'Nose rings – are they really such a big deal?'

One of these topics is too close to home – so close, it's moved in and has its feet up in my lounge.

But I won't tell the Journos that.

Was sure Adrian would put the kibosh on some of them, but I think his brain is full of Mucksted. He sent a short email saying, 'Please take the fine-toothcomb approach with everything they write.'

Asked the Journos if we wanted to co-opt the budding Year 9 Journo and got permission from his Head of Year to let him attend Second Lunch from next Friday so he can come.

Begged lift home from Sally with my full rucksack and extra bag of marking and planning.

'Come in for a cuppa,' I said.

'Off to York for a friend's hen weekend,' she said. 'Costing me three hundred pounds and I'll fail any Mucksted lesson observation. Be thankful you only get invited to funerals.'

Monday 4 December

Spouse went to Twickenham again this weekend, leaving me to catch up on all my marking in case Mucksted nose in anyone's books and folders. Son and DIL had friends staying over, so I didn't have to feel neglectful. I kept Radio 4 burbling away all weekend while I worked, too low to let it distract me, but high enough to pretend there was life on earth.

Ordered a takeaway on Saturday. Why is using Deliveroo called getting a takeaway and not ordering a bringhere?

Jim told me this morning that some heads of department had been in school on Sunday, getting the place ship-shape.

Why are we all in such a tizz? It's *pretend*!

Camilla certainly had a busy weekend compiling every email sent by the Smuts and forwarding them to us again 'in case you missed them first time'. Bahlul says that's twice he hasn't read them now.

In my free period, asked Auntie Google to find me the Mucksted consultants' website. According to them, if you thought Jesus was a miracle-worker, wait until you see us. The photographs are all air-brushed flawless people who look like the mannequins who wore the suits first.

Selected topics from the last round of speaking and listening assessments: 'Why school uniforms should be banned' (copied and pasted from one of the three million identical internet articles), 'Is it only girls who have eating disorders?' (a tear-jerker – the boy is as thin as string) and 'Life as a young carer' (her mother has MS).

The plagiarizer failed.

Resolutions Educational Consultants arrive at 8 a.m. tomorrow. The pupils know they're coming. All tutors told their forms this morning. Year 7 told me theirs had said there was nothing to be scared about as it was only a rehearsal, but she'd looked like death.

This evening, ate gammon, mash and peas, two portions of bread and butter pudding, and a bar of chocolate. Not sure why it's called comfort eating, as after dinner I had to undo my trousers.

Tuesday 5 December

Well, that day didn't turn out as expected.

In briefing, Adrian was meant to introduce us to the consultants. But they hadn't arrived.

They still weren't there for the start of Key Stage 3 assembly. Traffic problems.

When they did arrive, five minutes before end of assembly, I spotted them rushing into the hall. Two men and one woman – all in their twenties – looking very un-mannequin-like. One wore trainers.

Jim had all the rest of the gossip from, he claimed, Marion Coles and filled in the gaps for us. Apparently, they hadn't printed out paperwork either and were depending on smartphones and laptops to find the information school had sent. No one warned them our wi-fi signals at school are unreliable on all the days that have the word 'day' in them.

They observed maths and science lessons before break (phew), but one made an inappropriate comment to a pupil with learning difficulties. Another left a lesson halfway through for the toilet, and the pupils complained when he got back that he smelled of whisky. ('He stank the same as my dad.')

'You're kidding us now,' I said to Jim.

He said, 'Scout's honour.'

So, at break, Adrian called an emergency briefing in the staffroom. We all crowded in, standing embarrassingly close to each other, while he told us he'd asked the consultants to leave. 'I will be in touch with you all in due course,' Adrian said, smoothing his hands over his head. 'I can only apologize.'

Colleagues' faces were pale with sleeplessness and the thought of all the wasted work. 'We've just shortened our life spans for nothing,' said the Head of Geography to the back of my neck.

Once the shock wore off, though, lessons after break had a party atmosphere, as though we'd all found out we'd been given a wrong diagnosis and weren't going to peg it after all.

Camilla had cancelled the lunchtime meeting because of Mucksted, but she turned up to find us all in the office. She looked embarrassed. 'Sorry, team.'

Team?!

It's like a revolution. Collapse of class structures. The rise of the plebeians. All that stuff.

Wednesday 6 December

Went to bed at 9 last night and slept until 6. 'As if I'd been drugged,' I said to Mirror, stretching. 'I didn't know relief could do that.'

'One part relief, three parts Rioja can,' it said.

Can you get relief spots too? I've got three: forehead, left cheek, right cheek, as though someone who needs more tuition has been using my nose for target practice. Serves me right for sleeping through, letting the spots do their thing in the night without interruption.

The question everyone's asking at school is, 'Will there be another Mucksted?' As yet, Adrian ain't sayin' nuttin'. But there were blueberry muffins and cupcakes in the staffroom at break and a note saying, 'Your forbearance is much appreciated. Adrian.'

Jim took one of each in order to feel properly appreciated.

Started *The Road* with Year 13. Wrote the word 'apocalyptic' on the board. Conor said that he had a friend like that, but the tablets were improving things. Everyone laughed, thinking he'd made a joke.

Rebekah has read the entire novel and the rest of McCarthy's work. Didn't admit that I'd read none of his others. Where does she get the time while being a one-woman orchestra and reading the Pentateuch once a week?

'McCarthy's writing is like poetry,' she said. 'Isn't it? So beautiful and – and sparse. Like – winter on the page.'

The others gawped.

'You make my little English teacher heart go boom-diddy-boom,' I said. (Just you, Rebekah.)

Told people at Bible study about Rebekah's comment and how encouraged I'd been.

'Oooh, I must read *The Road* if it's so beautiful,' Jean said.

Probably should have mentioned the cannibalism and gore, but the moment had passed. I think she normally reads Catherine Cookson.

Thursday 7 December

Adrian has booked another Mucksted for Friday 19 January. He said in the email, 'It could potentially have been a longer wait had this company not had a cancellation.'

Cancellation? Well, if one school can come to its senses, why can't we?

This lot are called 'Innovation Education Professionals'. 'The name is pure poetry,' Jim said.

Went to the supermarket last night to buy a selection of fruit for Year 11 PHSE. When I came home, Spouse fished something out of the bag and said, 'What's this?'

'That's why I need to show fruit to teenagers,' I said. 'Because people grow up unable to recognize a kumquat.'

'Will school pay for these?' he said.

Pff!

In the lesson, Year 11 passed the fruits from hand to hand as though playing pass the parcel with a live grenade. 'You try it.' 'No, you try it.'

'I have knives here in case anyone wants to sample something,' I said.

One hand went up.

'I bet you'd all try a new flavour of Haribo if I brought some in,' I said, cutting up a starfruit for the adventurer.

Their faces lit up. 'Have you?'

'*No!*'

Year 7 Zak looked tired today. Angel Child asked if he was all right, but he stayed quiet.

Unwelcome submissions still arriving for the magazine. One wants to write about the day her hamster died. Her dad put it in the food recycling and she still has nightmares. Sent a kinder rejection note.

Samuel, the Year 9 Journo, came to the office to thank me and brought a selection of his writing. I think he was worried I didn't mean it and would need more proof. He's tiny. A little pocket student, smaller than most Year 7s. Looked him up on the system. A growth hormone disorder.

His writing, though? My goodness.

Year 7 parents' evening after school. I wanted to talk to Zak's mum especially, but she wasn't there.

Friday 8 December

Target practice spots have faded, replaced by something under my chin that Auntie Google thinks might qualify as a carbuncle. Spouse says to go to the doctor. But it's not true acne, is it? One spot one day, a few spots another. Even if they can be seen from space.

Jim reminded me this morning that Year 9 are on a GCSE-subjects taster day.

'Yes!' I said, punching the air.

Jim also reminded me that the timetabled teacher had to accompany them.

Endured a session on physics and understood 3 per cent of the words.

At lunchtime, introduced new-boy Samuel to the others. Had to remind Charlotte and Bella – who both said, 'Oh, he's so *cute*' – that they were not at Battersea, selecting a puppy.

Aleesha, Noora and Betsy are taking on research into bullying, dating and nose rings. Charlotte, Bella and Lukas are tackling homework and GCSEs. Also, I need to set up profile interviews with Colin and Marion, the deputy heads. Colin will definitely think it's revenge for not taking on my PHSE suggestions.

James and Samuel are compiling the Culture and Creativity section. They have bonded immediately, even though Samuel is the size of James's left arm. Drawn to each other's genius like magnets.

Phoned chosen printers in Warwick. Hope there's something for them to print. Adrian expects a pile of magazines by Friday 25 May, the day we break up for summer half-term.

Feel as though I'm at the base of Kilimanjaro with a handbag, flip-flops and a bag of boiled sweets.

Monday 11 December

The weekend was an improvement on the last. Babysat the Littluns on Saturday. Someone at church loved my song choices. Mirror was tolerably polite.

Slept only three hours last night though. Spent from 2 a.m. on the sofa, sipping tea. Was recalling something I'd heard at a teacher training session on behaviour years ago. Where were the notes?

Rummaged in a drawer and found them.

There it was. A list I'd admired because of its grammatical ingenuity but which hadn't touched me personally. At the time. 'The pained pass on pain. The yelled-at yell. The exploited exploit. The used use. The ignored ignore. The tortured torture. The bullied bully.'

Is that any excuse though? Does it absolve people from responsibility if their parents' lives are chaotic and they're neglected? Does it justify wielding power over those smaller and younger, the fact that you're only passing on what you received?

I remembered Miss Smith, the deputy head at my school in 1977, saying to me, 'We are trying to understand, bearing in mind your difficulties, but you are pushing us. We cannot have younger pupils scared to go into the girls' cloakrooms.' Cloakrooms. She meant toilets, but Miss Smith wouldn't have said that.

Made another cup of tea. Felt like drinking it deliberately hot to scald something away. I wasn't sure what.

Dozed for an hour, then woke with a stiff neck to hear my phone's alarm going off upstairs and Spouse batting at it as the cheery ringtone sang louder and louder.

At school, Year 11 moaned about writing a practice Paper 2 English Language. 'It's nearly Christmas,' they said.

'I'd hate to neglect my professional duties,' I said, 'however much I would like less marking.'

'We won't tell if you won't.'

'Just write.'

A smattering of Year 7s missed Period 5 lesson. Rehearsals for tomorrow's carol concert. 'Does Zak play an instrument?' I asked, scanning the room.

'No. Zak's bunking off,' someone said – someone I hope Zak doesn't count as a bosom friend. 'He'll be in the bogs playing games on his phone.'

Which he was.

Tuesday 12 December

Tired today. Woke at 5 and lay there waiting for the alarm and staring into the dark, thinking back to schooldays again. They're at my shoulder this week. Remembered Suzy turning to me in assembly when I was twelve and saying, 'Your clothes smell. And your mouth. Did you know?' And the teacher taking a lesson on hygiene who laughed at me for my lack of knowledge on basic routines. She'd looked disgusted. And the class had brayed.

'Why didn't you tell me?' I yelled at my mother, shaking her awake from a sherry stupor. 'Why haven't you shown me?'

Marion and Colin have agreed to be interviewed by the Journos. Marion saw me in the corridor today. 'Are these pupils trustworthy?' she said, her eyes twinkling. I do like her. If only she were the head-teacher and both deputies at once.

I said, 'Absolutely!' but crossed my fingers behind my back, sent up a quick prayer and thought back to my grandmother throwing salt over her shoulder. Hoped to cover all bases.

As we walked into briefing this morning, Bahlul nudged me. 'This time last week we were bricking it.'

Adrian was right behind him. 'I do hope not, Bahlul.'

Bahlul jumped.

Year 8 have written their own poems about conflict after our war poetry unit. One starts:

Me and my brother are always in conflict
How I wish we were always in nonflict

I gave the boy a merit. I love a new word.

Went to school carol concert, held in local church. Rebekah is a musical prodigy. Next time I lead worship, I must try not to think about her.

I feel inspired by the Year 8 poet to coin more words. Donflict: argy-bargy among professors. Oneflict: an argument with yourself. Goneflict: making up. Wontonflict: a fight over Chinese snacks.

Spouse has just said, sleepily, 'What the heck are you on about? What's "wontonflict"?'

Didn't realize I'd been saying them aloud.

Wednesday 13 December

Doctor's appointment at 9. Had filled in forms to sort out registration cover, asked Sally to take the beginning of my Year 12 class should I not get back in time, told a Year 13 who wanted coursework help in my free period that we'd have to postpone, and caught up with marking as much as I could.

Slept like a winter tortoise. And not a spot in sight. Even the carbuncle has done a bunk. A carbunkle.

Peered into Mirror. 'There must be something,' I said.

It tutted.

Sat bright-eyed and clear-skinned in front of doctor, and bottled it. Asked her to check a mole on my arm. 'I had one excised from my back five years ago,' I said.

'This large freckle?' she said, frowning. 'No, don't lose sleep over that.'

'Actually, about sleep . . .' I said.

But she'd already stood up.

Year 12 were finding Sally hugely absorbing when I puffed and panted into the classroom ten minutes into their lesson. I heard the laughter from the corridor. Olivia Private was gazing up at Sally as though she were a goddess.

'I've come to rescue you all from Miss Webb,' I said. 'I knew you'd miss me.'

School Christmas lunch today. Tradition says teachers sit with pupils, and the Smuts serve the lunch, wearing silly hats. Marion Coles wore a reindeer costume. Jim was dressed as Santa.

'Who got you involved?' I laughed, and pulled on his beard. 'You're not one of the Smuts.'

Sat at a table with some of my Year 11 form. They complained that this morning they'd been registered by Mr Vinnicombe, the drama teacher, and he'd made them revise from textbooks. 'You poor suffering children,' I said.

Not a bad Christmas lunch, if you don't count the stuffing balls like cannon shot and the tepid sprouts.

Year 13 finding *The Road* bleak and depressing. Good. Don't think McCarthy was looking for a career in farce. At least they've noticed.

Went to Bible study Christmas meal still full of cannon shot. But somehow forced down quiche, sausage rolls, pork pie, pasta salad, mince pies and chocolate cake.

Told Spouse he could kiss me anywhere on my spotless face tonight without risking a gobful of toothpaste.

Romeo and Juliet, stand aside.

Thursday 14 December

A spot. Only, not a spot. A major eruption. Side of nose.

'Do. Not. Speak,' I said to Mirror, while layering on concealer with the fish slice.

Year 11 PHSE class asked, 'Are we having fruit again? We loved it.'

Only in my dreams did they ask that. They really wanted to know, 'Is it Haribo week?'

'No, we're doing saturated fats.' Displayed Colin's first slide. A picture of a Grand Big Mac and chips with a Twix McFlurry.

'Ohhhhhhh!' A groan of pleasure escaped from some.

'Urrggh!' went others.

Recruited someone from 'ohhhhhh' faction and someone from 'urrggh' faction to work on a debate piece about teenagers' eating habits for *Beauchamp Matters*. And both can spell and punctuate! Bonus!

Really odd. Hurtled into English office during Year 8's lesson before lunch as I'd forgotten to take their marked books. Camilla was there, putting a pill on her tongue and about to gulp water. Her face changed to dark red. Like a sudden sunset.

'A headache?' I said, straightening the pile of books. 'Hope the pills work.'

She put the bottle in her bag, nodded 'Thanks' and left the room. Followed her heels down the stairs and corridor. Clack clack clack.

The side of my nose is lathered in toothpaste tonight. Looks like a mountain from which the sun has melted the snow on one slope only.

Friday 15 December

In a just world, we'd have finished for Christmas today. But we must slog on for another week until the 22nd. It was written on the wearied faces of teachers and pupils passing me in my break duty corridor. Enthusiasm erased, bit by bit, by the rubber of an eight-week half-term.

Son, DIL and Littluns are coming over for Christmas Day. The Isleworth daughters are arriving Boxing Day with sleeping bags and a giant Christmas cake.

When am I supposed to buy presents? Make mince pies? Pop to the shops for Sellotape to later find five rolls I'd forgotten about in a drawer?

Bahlul says he's going shopping this weekend.

'No chance I'll be doing that,' I said. 'This weekend I'm finishing all my marking so there's none to do at Christmas. Apart from Year 13 coursework drafts. And Year 11 essays. And some Year 7 true stories I'll keep until last as a treat to have with Baileys.'

Year 7 have read the chapter in *Boy* in which the young Dahl puts goat's droppings in his sister's boyfriend's pipe, and written their own stories about pranks they have inflicted or suffered from. Zak told us he once put dog poo in his sister's bed. We believed him.

At least he seems a bit more cheerful.

The Journos are on it like a Shakespeare sonnet, I told them. They've interviewed Colin and Marion, and spent today's session drafting the profile pieces. James and Samuel have met together three times since last week to plan and write. Lukas says the Head of Games will help with gathering sports reports.

Checked all the plans and advised adjustments. They want to meet again next Thursday lunchtime, as on Friday we finish early.

'Run that by me again,' I said. 'You want an extra Journos?'

They beamed. I promised to bring mega-chocolate.

Monday 18 December

The Littluns helped put our tree up on Saturday afternoon. Tinsel has been forced on us.

Marked like a demon this weekend. Rewarded myself with three Maltesers per piece of work, then moved on to a box of Milk Tray until – ugh! – only soft ones left.

Then remembered the half-termly grades for all classes and ate the soft ones while inputting the grades.

Overall, the work took twice as long as expected. Was hoping to develop some more article pitches. Bye, bye, writing career.

Spouse has downloaded Christmas meditations. Found him downstairs at 6.30 this morning still in pyjamas, eyes closed, listening to the Nativity story. 'And there were shepherds. An angel of the Lord appeared to them . . .'

I cleared my throat.

He tapped his tablet and jumped up. 'Shall I make toast?'

I checked my watch.

'Don't give me that,' he said.

Almost snapped back, but it felt rude after silencing the angels in the middle of announcing the Messiah's birth.

We ate toast and listened while the shepherds went to see Jesus.

I missed the bus and had to walk, carrying all the marking.

Camilla was in the office. She looked particularly groomed and made up, I thought, as I wiped sweat off my brow, blew my nose noisily and off-loaded all the marking on to my desk.

Too made up.

She asked whether I could pass work on to Year 12 and Year 13 for her tomorrow. Didn't explain why.

Year 11 not happy in their double lesson. 'It's the last week. You can't make us do a Question 4,' they said.

I told them it was the hardest question on the paper so they needed more practice.

'Will you bring us sweets on Thursday, our last lesson?'

'If you work on Question 4 without whinging today,' I said.

Sigh. Huff. Puff. Sigh.

I said, 'It's like a busy morning on the lung ward in here.'

Tuesday 19 December

Rebekah came to the English office at break to submit an extra essay. More marking! But I can't say, 'Stop making such an effort.'

'Good weekend, Miss?' she said, while she wrote her name on the essay.

Dilemma.

Then she said, 'Our church had a Christmas service. I sang.'

Go on – say it, you wuss, I told myself. 'S-so did mine. I sang too,' I said.

'Oh!' She was clearly reappraising me.

Jim came in, so I stood to usher Rebekah out before she mentioned anything else about religion. From faithful disciple to chicken in three seconds. Felt ashamed. My spiritual conscience took the form of the God-lady at church, wagging a gnarled finger. Heretical, surely, replacing God in my mind with an old woman from Bishop's Tachbrook.

Year 8 wrote Christmas poems in the computer room. The brief was to evoke a traditional Christmas scene. But they refused to write in free verse, thinking rhyme and plodding rhythm mandatory. Lynne and I gave in and showed them rhyme-generating websites, but one boy, desperate for a rhyme for satsumas, had to include some wild cats in his Christmas scene.

Some of Year 12 tried to convince me it was their last lesson of the term. Chloe Private said, checking her planner, 'No, that's Friday Period 3. We go home after lunch, though, so it's a half-day.'

'Shut up, Chloe,' one said.

They're clearly planning to be gravely ill on Friday.

Worked them harder than ever on the history of punctuation marks. The Privates lapped it up.

'Just in case,' I said, 'I'll set your Christmas homework now. And here's some work from Miss Stent too.'

The inevitable groans.

No Camilla meant no lunchtime meeting. 'I'll give you a top tip,' Jim said. 'Pudding today is apple pie.'

Followed him to the dining hall like a faithful dog.

Wednesday 20 December

Spouse has upped his power walking from thirty minutes to forty-five. Meanwhile, I've put on another pound. That'll be the Maltesers, Milk Tray and apple pie diet, the one Hollywood hasn't hit on yet. If Spouse gets thinner and thinner while I get fatter and fatter, one day someone will see me alone in the street and think I've nibbled away my own husband.

Had my hair cut yesterday after school. There's definitely more grey. I asked how much it cost per year to keep your hair un-greyed.

That's that decision made, then. I'll stay old-haired and solvent.

Camilla not back in school now until next term, we're told. Again, no one knows anything. Or if they do, they're not saying. The department does feel like a lighter place. But we've got used to her, as one does a wart or arthritis. So it felt strange eating Sally's puff-pastry mince pies and not feeling remorse about the crumbs on the office carpet.

Year 13 brought Tesco cakes and silly hats. 'I honestly couldn't eat another thing,' I said, accepting a huge chunk of coffee and walnut on a piece of kitchen towel.

Rebekah brought reindeer-shaped vegan biscuits. I let the incongruity pass by and ate a small one.

Then we analysed McCarthy's use of monochrome in evoking an apocalyptic, ravaged landscape and developing themes of destruction and death. 'Happy Christmas, Miss,' they said as they left, and Conor blew a party horn.

Marked Rebekah's extra essay tonight before Spouse and I went to the pub to celebrate having free Wednesday evenings during the Bible study's Christmas break. Fantastic comparison of Atwood and McCarthy from Rebekah. I couldn't have written it.

Still, she made a bad call on the reindeer biscuits.

Thursday 21 December

Christmas Jumper Day at school.

'Will this do?' I asked Mirror.

'It's a red jumper. What more can I say?'

'Does it look Christmassy?' I said.

Mirror said that, combined with a Santa hat, Christmas pudding earrings and some tinsel round my neck, it would look Christmassy.

'That's not happening,' I said. 'I hate festooning myself.'

'No danger today,' it said.

Bahlul, Sally and Jim were all in tasteless, garish, festoony Christmas jumpers.

Year 11 wanted to know if we were watching the Muppets' version of *A Christmas Carol* in our English lesson.

'Why would we?' I said.

Because it was their last English lesson. And because they'd watched the first half in maths.

'It's still a no,' I said. 'But the work I've planned is Christmas-themed, I promise.'

I'd found two non-fiction texts to compare: a scene from *Angela's Ashes* about the family's Christmas dinner and a news article about the work of Shelter, the homeless charity, at Christmas.

They said they weren't fooled. 'This is exam practice for Paper 2, isn't it?'

'I did bring sweets,' I replied. 'But I need whole-class cooperation for forty-five minutes before I give them out.'

They settled down as though accepting the inevitable and we read the texts together.

'I am so depressed,' said Danny as soon as we'd read the last sentence. He put his head in his hands. Others agreed and accused me of ruining their Christmas with true accounts of people in dire circumstances.

Had to give the sweets out early.

Later, wasn't surprised to see two girls missing from the Journos session at lunch. The rest of us cracked on, sustained by Celebrations and chocolate cookies. Slowly, slowly, like a dot-to-dot picture that gradually becomes defined and clear, a magazine seems possible.

'Did you get bullied at school, Miss?' Noora asked me.

The others turned, listening.

I said, 'No, I didn't.'

'Mrs Coles told us any bully she's ever dealt with has been insecure, even though they look confident,' Noora said.

Said I agreed with Mrs Coles and offered round the chocolates again.

Every class asked why I wasn't wearing a Christmas jumper.

Friday 22 December

Two spots, a grey eyebrow hair and a restless night: special treats for the last day of term.

Registration was all wrapping paper and breakfasting on chocolate Santas, then I dragged my form to the Christmas assembly for Years 10 and 11. They were noisy – high on end-of-term – and even Adrian's shushing and shisshing went unnoticed.

In Period 1, Year 7 were equally jumpy. I'd made a word search with all their names in it. (Genius, Lynne said. I'll have that one.) It quietened them until someone found 'sex' in it and they were off again.

Zak very subdued, though.

'What's up?' I said.

He told me his mum and dad have separated. Zak and his sister are with his mum. 'My dad's taken Oscar,' he said.

'Oscar?'

'Our spaniel.'

The Head of Year 7 passed me while I was on break duty and trying to stop pupils being happy. I flagged her down. Had she heard about Zak's family?

No, she hadn't. She scurried along the corridor towards an awkward phone call.

Jim's Year 9 read Christmas cracker jokes and decided what made them funny aka detailed linguistic analysis of humour. 'Thanks for the fun lesson, Miss,' they said. 'We thought you'd make us do work.'

Seven Year 12s missing. The remaining seven – three Privates and four not – read an extract from *A Christmas Carol* and identified language change features. Chloe Private brought giant Christmas cookies from Waitrose. Everyone took one. No one asked her to shut up.

End-of-term staff lunch in the dining hall once classrooms were tidy and the last pupils had disappeared, trailing tinsel. Three staff moving to new jobs. One retiring. We listened to speeches, clapped, and envied the retiree.

Polly dropped me home. 'Any presents from pupils?' she said in the car, nodding towards my heavy rucksack.

'Nope,' I said. 'I bet you got some, though.'

'Nope. Me neither.'

Felt unreasonably happy and full of goodwill.

Tomorrow I'm hitting the shops like a ball from Nadal's racquet.

First half of spring term

Monday 8 January

January's teacher training day. The alarm rang at 6. Spouse had forgotten to alter the central heating timer, so I showered and dressed while my teeth chattered.

So long as *they're* having a lovely time.

Stollen and hot chocolate for breakfast, standing by the oven turned up to Gas 9. Spouse still in bed. 'No point gardening frozen ground,' he'd said last night.

The house was warming up as I put my coat on.

Walked to bus with my feet numb, past cars iced with frost like ghosts in the street and skeletal corpses of Christmas trees in front gardens.

Sally gave me a hug when I entered the office. 'How was your Christmas?'

'Over,' I said.

'It isn't. Want some calories?'

I said, 'No, but yes.'

She'd brought in half a Christmas cake and some chocolate biscuits.

Camilla came in then. Sally said, 'Help yourself to any of this, Camilla.'

She won't. But I wish she would. Her thick woollen jacket can't disguise her thinness.

Today's offering from Adrian: in-house (cheap) PowerPoint presentations from colleagues.

Session 1: Colin on emotional intelligence. Delivery like an automaton.

Break: coffee and plain biscuits. No flapjacks. Jim hyperventilated and ran upstairs for Sally's Christmas cake.

Session 2: the Head of Languages on creating inclusive class-rooms. Not bad, except that there are always disgraced pupils standing outside hers. And her session was meant to be forty-five minutes to allow for departmental meetings. She took an hour and ten.

Lunch: the baked potatoes left over from September's teacher training day.

Session 3: Marion with a comedy routine about how to foster a positive classroom climate. We applauded like crazed seals.

Training day finished at 3.30. Stayed at school until 6. Waited for bus for fifty minutes getting frostbite. Happy new year to me.

Tuesday 9 January

Last night's dream: I'm on the bus going the wrong way. I try to ring Camilla, but my phone is a flapjack. The inside of the bus is an apocalyptic landscape. The Littluns appear. 'Grandma!'

Said to Sally when I arrived in the office, 'I forgot to ask how your Christmas was. You distracted me with carbohydrates.'

She sighed. 'It was good, then bad, then good,' she said. 'Started the holidays engaged to Archie, then we split, then we were engaged again.'

'Oh.'

'It's all fine,' she said. 'A misunderstanding, really. Come on, better get to briefing.'

Adrian began with, 'I said all I wanted to yesterday.' But then found plenty else. We all sat thinking about our unphotocopied photocopying.

Afterwards, he caught me as I left and asked me to make an appointment sometime soon to update him on the magazine. Arrggh! Am seeing him tomorrow morning in my free period.

Year 8 looked intrigued as I gave out copies of Philip Pullman's dramatic adaptation of *Frankenstein*.

'What's it about, Miss?'

'Someone who collects body parts from corpses and sews them together to make a hideous creature that comes alive.'

One or two looked dubious or alarmed, but the front row sat up. Cheap trick, but works every time.

Year 7 wrote about their Christmas holidays. A minute after I'd announced the task, I remembered about Zak and the kind of Christmas he might have had. Too late. He already had his head bent and was writing.

Spouse was out for his power walk when I got home at 6.30. When he came back, his legs were blue.

'Shorts?' I said. 'In these temperatures? You have no blood below the waist.'

He said he didn't *feel* cold.

'Dying mountaineers say the same,' I said.

He's taking this far too seriously.

Wednesday 10 January

No spots so far, and over Christmas my skin was much clearer. Spouse is using it as a reason to resurrect the part-time debate. 'This happens every holiday,' he said.

'I still spent four days doing schoolwork,' I said.

'In a warm, quiet study with a ready supply of coffee and biscuits. It's not the same.'

'And I read a novel,' I said. He'd bought me *The Kite Runner* at Christmas. I'd spent a whole day with it, my heart alert to its pain.

He said he wouldn't congratulate me, because I *should* be reading novels, and not just for school purposes.

Showed Zak's 'My Christmas' account to Sally before registration. 'The poor kid,' she said, looking up from his book. 'What kind of Christmas is that for an eleven-year-old?'

'I know. No Christmas at all.'

I was thinking that surely, somewhere in my own memory, there must be one childhood Christmas that didn't involve yelling or spilt sherry or someone packing a suitcase?

But I didn't say that to Sally.

Had email from Adrian, postponing our meeting until my free on Friday.

Some of Year 12 hadn't done their Christmas homework, predictably. (Not you, Privates.) Wasn't feeling merciful. Kept them behind at break while I typed their misdemeanours into SIMS and made them watch. Bunking the last day. Late homework. Inattention.

'Gosh, you're on a mish today, Miss,' one girl said, which she wouldn't have been able to say drunk or, if she were Adrian, into a microphone.

Year 13 double lesson: detailed study of the characterization of the young boy in *The Road*, especially the way he tries to help his father in dire circumstances. 'He's so vulnerable but so strong,' Rebekah said dreamily.

'Just like me,' Conor said, like a pin to a balloon.

Thursday 11 January

First spots of the term. Angry ones, as though miffed at being suppressed over Christmas. Trying a new dab-on remedy I saw advertised in a women's magazine when I was at the doctor's surgery last month. It cost £21.95. The bottle looks like the ones ear drops come in. In fact, I probably could fit it in my ear.

'Does Spouse know how much you paid?' Mirror said.

Told Mirror that if I needed a financial advisor, I would hire one.

Bible study started last night, but Year 11 full reports are due next week. Said to Spouse, 'Tell them I have thirty in the class and each report takes twenty minutes to compile.'

He was sure I didn't need to justify my absence. They'd understand.

I said to tell them anyway.

This half-term's PHSE topic? Bullying. 'We've done this topic every single year,' the class complained.

'Which must mean', I said, 'that no one is spiteful in Year 11, if it's been successful. There are no fights. No one sends nasty messages. No one spreads rumours. No one terrorizes little Year 7s in the toilets.'

Silence.

'Hm. Thought so,' I said.

One girl turned to another. 'Terrorizing Year 7s in the toilets, though? What's *wrong* with people?'

Three Year 11s from my English class earned break-time detention for producing no Christmas homework.

'I worked four whole days over Christmas,' I said. But it was like water off a duck's (buttered) back.

Gave Year 7 their marked Christmas writing. 'Can we read some out?' they asked, as I knew they would. Zak stood and read his to a room as quiet as a sanctuary. When he sat down again, Angel Child patted him.

Spouse out tonight, having a drink with Son. I wrote more Year 11 reports until 9, then found the Baileys and looked for something happy to watch on TV.

Friday 12 January

I am not transformed. The advert in the women's magazine lied.

The office phone was ringing when I arrived. It was Zak's form tutor, asking me to keep an eye on him. He may need to go to a foster home, at least temporarily. His mum is in breakdown.

He did look white-faced in Period 1, I noticed, and his hair was uncombed.

Jim's Year 9 begged for more Christmas joke-writing.

'It's January,' I said.

'Can we write more jokes at Easter then?'

Explained that the crucifixion didn't lend itself so well to comedic interpretation.

Adrian hasn't lost his list, I found out in our meeting. I tried to make the Journos sound committed to showing the school in its best light.

'Dating schoolfriends, though?' he said. 'A bit – shallow, as a topic?'

Pointed out that he had agreed to that one by email. 'I promise,' I said, 'I'll make sure no shallowness is allowed. That one raises some important issues, in fact.'

'I've other fish to fry, to be honest.' He sighed. 'I'm sure you'll do the school proud.' He did that head-smoothing thing with his hands.

I so very almost nearly said the word 'Mucksted'.

Full complement of Journos. They'd all said they would work on articles over Christmas. Apart from James and Samuel, they didn't. But the boys have press-ganged their more reliable friends to produce reviews.

'Email them to me,' I said. 'I'll have a look. And thank you.'

They hadn't finished. 'We also wondered about a writing competition,' James said. 'Our class did some mini-sagas with Mr Jones. You know – a story in fifty words.' He looked at Noora to back him up. 'Didn't we?' he said.

Her eyes widened. *We did?*

Samuel said, 'We could pick a theme. Say, aeroplanes.'

'Aeroplanes?' the others chorused. (Not you, James.)

'What about relationships as a theme?' I suggested. 'It'd link with others. The bullying. Dating.'

They leapt on this.

Mini-saga competition. Why didn't I think of that?

Monday 15 January

Son, DIL and Littluns round for lunch yesterday. Grandgirl helped me make apple crumble. DIL said she remembered helping her grandmother with cooking too.

Why does the word 'grandmother' make me feel fossilized?

It doesn't help that when we play Uno, Grandboy has to keep saying, 'Grandma, it's your turn. Grandma, you didn't say "Uno". Grandma, you're dribbling on your cards.'

In my free period, sifted through the emails James and Samuel forwarded – reviews of books, plays, computer games, films – and created a file called 'Culture and Creativity' in the *Beauchamp Matters* folder. Quality of submissions varied. Some well written but with atrocious spelling and punctuation. Sent them back, demanding corrections. Some with exemplary spelling and punctuation but little idea of the rules of review-writing. Sent them back with a rejection. One review of *To Kill a Mockingbird* said, 'They find Tom Robinson guilty.'

Need some reviews by girls. James and Samuel's social milieu is limited.

A lesson on genre for Year 8, before we start reading the *Frankenstein* play.

'But *why* is it called gossip fiction?' a girl asked.

'Gothic,' I said.

'Try listening,' Goater said to her. Goater isn't learning very fast about how to win friends and influence people.

Poor Year 11. It's back to English Language Paper 1 for more practice. 'We'll go over the structure question again,' I said. 'We haven't quite cracked it.'

Groan.

I said, 'Look, does anyone have an elastic hairband I can use?'

They frowned. *What's she up to?* Someone in the front row pulled one from her hair and passed it to me.

'Right. Watch me stretch this,' I said. 'Who thinks I'll let it snap?'

Stretch.

They watched.

Stretch.

Eyes widened.

Stretch stretch stretch.

Some winced.

Stretch. Stretch.

One tiny scream from a girl.

I relaxed the band and a relief sigh wisped round the classroom.

'*That* is tension,' I said. 'It's what writers achieve with structural methods such as foreshadowing, delayed information, repetition – all the terms on your list.' I asked someone to give out copies of M. R. James's ghost story *Rats*. 'Let's see how this writer does it.'

The girl whose hairband I'd used said she was feeling really tense already.

'Why?' I said.

'You've put my hairband in your pocket and I don't know if I'm getting it back.'

One week left until Mucksted II.

Tuesday 16 January

Year 8 were tricksy. They tried to divvy out the cast of *Frankenstein*, but everyone wanted to be the monster made of body parts. Served me right for asking for volunteers. I saw Lynne's eyebrows rise as I did it. I wrenched back control and chose Leon, green board pen spoiler boy. I saw him in a drama production last year.

Goater is playing Dr Frankenstein, which figures.

Year 12 are doing mock exams this week. Remembered Jim's advice and sat at the back. It clearly worried them. They kept looking over their shoulders. At one point, Gus Private caught me mid-yawn and I hadn't even put my hand over my mouth, thinking myself safe.

Camilla's Top Tips #6 built on the Head of Languages' training about inclusive classrooms. 'Let's all offer one strategy we use to make every child in the room feel empowered,' Camilla said, her eyes bright with something or other – reading Adrian's blog, perhaps.

Jim said, 'Teach them something they didn't know before?'

'Yes!' she said, as though he'd invented the internet or something.

Some in the Year 13 class had finished improving their course-work drafts and gave them in today. I tried to make the rest feel empowered. 'You can do this. You totally can. One more push.'

It works in *Call the Midwife*. It was worth a shot.

Wednesday 17 January

Why have I never learned in sixteen years of teaching? Each free period, as with today Period 1, I start with wild ambitions. A pile of thirty exercise books. A folder-full of Year 13 essays comparing *The Road* with *The Handmaid's Tale*. *C'mon*, I tell myself. *Fire up the purple pen. Get into the zone.* But when the bell goes, I've marked a third of my intentions. Even using Camilla's Top Tips. Even ignoring Bahlul.

'Sorry,' I said to Year 13 in the lesson. 'I'll get them marked asap.'

All round the room, except for Rebekah, a communal shrug, like a Mexican wave but with shoulders.

Conor said, 'You can leave mine as long as you like. Getting it back will depress me.'

'I *want* to know my marks,' Rebekah said.

'Thirty out of thirty,' the rest intoned, and she blushed.

Started planning for Mucksted II on Friday. Good news: I have four lessons, not five as last time. Bad news: it's Year 8's last lesson on a Friday and Camilla says I can't let Mucksted observe a reading lesson. 'It's not all *silent* reading,' I said. 'We do verbal book reviews, or analyse blurbs, or watch an author on YouTube, or –'

'I'd stay with *Frankenstein*,' she said.

Be my guest, Camilla. I'll buy you a one-way ticket.

Year 11 reports are due in at 4 p.m. on Friday, which is also Mucksted II day, which is also Journos day. Bearing that in mind, missed Bible study again and stayed up until 1 a.m. to finish the reports.

Said to Spouse, 'Tell Bible study people that –'

'I know,' he said.

Writing this, I realize it's now tomorrow.

Thursday 18 January

Slept from 2.30 a.m. until 4.30 a.m. At 6, my face looked like a non-face.

'No one could accuse you of flattery,' I said to Mirror.

'Just doing my job,' it said.

'Try to do it worse.'

Colin's prescribed PHSE lesson was a link to a patronizing documentary about bullying that had clearly been designed for primary schools. Searched YouTube for an alternative. Found one about a bullying experiment that tested whether people would stop if they saw someone being victimized. Most didn't stop.

It was harrowing, clearly *not* designed for primary schools. Kept an eye on the door and my finger near 'Pause' in case any Smuts came by.

Tuesdays and Thursdays are Literature lessons this term for Year 11. The Monday doubles will focus on Language. 'We're revising unseen poetry today,' I announced, 'for Literature Paper 2.'

'What's "unseen poetry" again?' one asked. Someone always does.

Reminded them it meant poetry they hadn't encountered before.

'So, if we haven't seen it, how do we write about it?'

Tried to keep my voice gentle. 'Poetry you haven't seen *until* it turns up on the exam paper.'

'Can you tell us which poem it will be?'

Said it would mean doing something illegal.

'But you want us to pass, don't you?'

In Year 8's lesson, after the boy playing Captain Walton had delivered the Prologue, I broke the news about the cancelled reading lesson. 'So tomorrow we might have observers watching Dr Frankenstein and Clerval begin Act 1. Make sure you bring your plays.'

'Will they see me as the monster?' Leon asked.

'Not sure we'll reach that bit,' I said.

Adrian arranged for school to stay open until 9 so that staff could prepare for Mucksted. There must be an award for that level of altruism.

Friday 19 January

Camilla admitted she'd been told Mucksted might visit the Journos at lunchtime.

She admitted this after they'd been.

Two male consultants in their forties and sporting impeccable suits arrived ten minutes in. Thanks, gentlemen, for transforming my group of chatty, lively teenagers, tapping keyboards and correcting each other's grammar, into tongue-tied, stiff-backed, blushing adolescents.

The consultants asked me questions about the magazine and its aims. I hoped Adrian hadn't passed on his list. James and Samuel showed them, shyly, some of the work they've collected, and they read one of Samuel's quirky reviews. 'I used to teach English,' one of the men said. 'That's outstanding writing for a Year 9.'

An English teacher? Help!

'Hello again,' he said later when he arrived halfway through my Year 8 lesson. Goater was playing Frankenstein. She had borrowed an Einstein-type wig from Drama, which had slipped to one side, and she and the boy playing Clerval were in chairs in the middle of the room. The rest of the class were arranged around the edge, making notes on characterization, supposedly.

The two actors held plastic cups filled with blackcurrant juice.

'It's not real wine, Sir,' said Clerval, nodding towards the cup as the consultant took a seat near him. 'But cheers, anyway.'

'That's not in the script,' Frankenstein said. 'Your next line is, "You don't say."'

Leon interrupted from where he sat. 'I'm the monster, Sir. But I'm not alive yet. Are you coming back Monday?'

The man made a note.

'Resume normal service, please, cast,' I said.

Eh?

'Carry *on.*'

Discovered later that Mucksted observed Camilla and Bahlul too. Sally and Jim escaped. Jim said he'd slipped Marion a bribe. We weren't sure if it was a joke.

So tired, but not sure I'll sleep. Spouse and I over-ordered on take-away curry. Enough for four. But wastefulness is a sin, and even more so if it's chicken Madras.

Monday 22 January

In the bathroom most of Friday night and Saturday with diarrhoea like a lava stream, wondering how feasible it would be to set up a desk in there. 'Must have been the curry/Mucksted combination,' I said to Spouse. We both agreed that it didn't sound pleasant.

He went alone to church and from there to Son and DIL's. We'd been invited to Sunday lunch. I stayed home alone all day, tackled schoolwork and ate dry toast and cream crackers.

Every cloud. Bathroom Scales said this morning, 'You've lost two pounds. Congratulations.'

Mirror said, 'It'll go on again once she's back on the pies.'

'Excuse me,' I said. 'I am here, in the room.'

Had forgotten to submit Year 11 reports on Friday. Sent them when I arrived at school this morning, hoping no one would notice they were late.

Adrian called an extra briefing before school. Apparently, Mucksted II's prediction is that Ofsted might, just, at a pinch, rate us as Good. Not an overwhelming endorsement.

Zak is now in a foster home. Says his mum has been sectioned. He comes to school in a taxi now from the other side of Coventry. 'Takes twenty-five minutes, Miss.' He passed me a creased sheet of paper. 'Enough time to write my English homework.'

Zak must be torn, wondering who is parenting him. At least I only had to wonder that for three months before Mum took all her Valium with a bottle of sherry and my foster placement went from temporary to permanent overnight.

Tuesday 23 January

Email from Camilla. Kindly submit your reports by the deadlines, otherwise the world will end.

Started language diversity topics with Year 12. Introduced them to idiolects. 'You all have one,' I said. 'The individual way you speak. Your accent, dialect, the way you use tone or pitch, or how fast you talk, or how often you say "like" or "sort of".' I turned to the computer. 'I'll show you a David Crystal clip on idiolect, but only if you promise to pay him proper respect.'

Teenagers will do anything for a bit of video. 'O blessed be his holy name,' they chanted.

Gus Private and Chloe Private both indignantly claimed they never use 'like' as a filler, as though we'd accused them of body odour. The others spent the lesson trying to catch them out.

Gus fell first. Chloe soon after.

Tried not to feel they deserved it, but it was, like, sort of, like, hard not to.

At lunchtime, Camilla passed on Mucksted's comments about the English department. Apparently, our lessons were varied, well pitched and engaging.

Yay, we said.

But the quality of marking across the department, seen in pupils' books and on displays, was inconsistent.

Bahlul looked at his knees.

And, Camilla said to me later, the consultant wondered whether I should have allowed a wider range of pupils to act out the parts in *Frankenstein* in the interests of equality.

'What? A new monster each lesson?' I said. 'That would cause confusion. And some of them can't act. And some faint if asked.'

Told Jim what the consultant had said. 'What a load of garbage people talk,' he said, which was a comfort.

Wednesday 24 January

Gave Year 12 their mock exam papers back. Gus got full marks and announced it in such a patronizing tone that another boy said, 'I'd rather fail than be a moron.' I told him off, and the atmosphere was as taut as a bootlace the entire lesson.

Year 13 lessons are frustrating, constantly undermined by those who won't do the preparatory reading. 'I don't understand,' I said. 'Why did you sign up for English Literature if you don't like reading?' (Not you, Rebekah.)

They didn't know there'd be so much. Quite so often. Analysed in so much detail.

Matt wasn't in the lesson. Conor told me, 'He got busted.'

I asked what kind of busted.

'The ganja again,' he said. 'Excluded for a week this time.'

At last. A proper punishment. Made mental note to send him work, but then Conor said Matt had gone to Morocco with his dad.

Went to Camilla's classroom during my free in Period 5 to give her some Year 12 resources she'd left by the photocopier. Thought she'd need them for their lesson. No one there. A note on the desk read, 'Miss Stent has had to go home. Please revise quietly in the library.'

Went to Bible study without Spouse, who'd gone to a lecture about horticulture. I arrived late after finishing Year 7 marking. Dinner was two Weetabix.

Walked into the host's lounge to a teasing, light-hearted chorus of 'Oh, who's this?' 'Is she new?' 'Has she been before?'

'Oh, ha ha,' I said. Landed moodily in a chair and the room went still. Had to apologize. And then they asked me how work was and fed me cookies.

Mercy is hard to take.

Thursday 25 January

Bathroom Scales said this morning, 'Two pounds back on, I'm afraid.'

'I think it's the two cookies last night,' I said.

'They weighed a pound each?' said Mirror.

Refused to look at Mirror after that. Brushed my teeth with eyes shut.

Emails already appearing about impending Ofsted visit. Not even a week's break after Mucksted. It's like going back for dental treatment when the swellings haven't gone down from the last appointment.

Jim has coined the term Sodoffsted, after amending it from something worse that Bahlul suggested.

'I'm telling on you two,' I said.

But Camilla wasn't in. Again.

The Head of Psychology, Miss Singh, took the Year 11 assembly. She doesn't look old enough to be a teacher, let alone a Head of something. She told her own story about being bullied at school and how it affected her. Poignant and upsetting, so some pupils in tears.

Straight into PHSE, and the same topic. Colin's PowerPoint slides were about different forms of bullying. Physical. Social media. Gossip. Cliques.

Year 11 clearly see me and young Miss Singh as different species. 'Did they have bullying in your day too?' one asked me.

'Of course,' I said. 'The kids in the cave next door to ours were mean.'

They took way too long to catch on.

'Seriously, though, Miss. Did you get bullied?'

'I did,' I said. I didn't add that this had been at home, not school.

Told Sally about the mini-saga competition. She offered to administrate and judge it.

'You don't have to,' I said. 'If it's too much –'

She covered her ears. 'I can't hear you.'

Later, she said, 'Anyway, I need to keep busy. Please let me help.'

Friday 26 January

Camilla back today, but as pale as a spectre.

In Year 7's lesson, Zak told me he'd visited his mum in hospital yesterday after school. She'd looked weird. Kind of asleep, but not. Slurry voice.

It brought back a memory of a dark corridor and people in loose dressing gowns. My mother, in an old person's chair, her eyes focused on something, someone, else.

Said to Zak, 'Your mum will have loved your visit.'

Jim's Year 9s have been nagging him to let them write jokes. 'You must stop that,' I said to them. 'Mr Jones needs to teach you Shakespeare.'

'Ugh!'

I said, 'Anyway, Shakespeare plays have jokes.'

Incredulous looks.

Wondered if I'd got it wrong about which text they're studying. Which one had Mr Jones chosen? One of the tragedies? *Macbeth*? *Romeo and Juliet*?

No, they said. *As You Like It*.

'That's a comedy,' I said.

Incredulous looks.

Only Samuel and James at Journos. The rest missing – a combo of illness, detentions and, for Lukas, a sports event. Too many days like that and we'll get behind.

The two boys performed their usual ritual on arrival. James lowers his computer chair so that he's not typing from a great height with his arms dangling, and Samuel raises his to maximum so that he can see the keyboard.

Told them Miss Webb was taking on the mini-sagas.

'Will she let us help her?' James said.

'I'd imagine so,' I said.

They punched the air. 'Yes!'

Tried not to look put out.

Four friends round for dinner tonight. 'Hey, you're looking trim,' one of them said to Spouse as they took off their coats in the hall and handed over bottles of wine.

He told them about his walking as we ate steak and jacket potatoes later.

'You're an example to us all!' they said.

I lathered more butter on my potato and mashed it in good and proper.

Monday 29 January

Babysat on Saturday evening. Grandboy read a *Biff, Chip & Kipper* book to me and I filled in his reading diary: 'He coped very well with the new vocabulary, sounding the words out. Grandma.'

It gave me an idea. So, once the Littluns had settled, emailed the editor at *emagazine*. She'd liked my previous articles. Would she take one about the use of reading diaries in primary schools? I thought it would be helpful for her audience of A-level English teachers and students.

Stayed awake much of Saturday night wondering what I'd do if she said yes. When would I write it?

Acceptance email this morning: 1,500 words by the end of April. That's three months, so 500 words each month. Approximately seventeen words a day.

Chopped up into bits, it's easily dealt with, as Sweeney Todd also discovered.

Showed Year 8 the original passage from Mary Shelley's novel in which the monster comes alive so that they could compare it with the Pullman dramatization for schools. 'Why didn't she write it like Pullman in the first place,' one boy wanted to know, 'instead of all this waffle?'

'That's not waffle,' I said. 'It's nineteenth-century Gothic fiction. Prose of the highest order. Highly respected.'

He raised his eyebrows and they spelled the word 'sceptic'.

The upside: Leon is a changed boy now that I have allowed him to be a monster legitimately.

Mustn't forget to start writing Year 13 reports, due next week. How come, on my own school reports, my 1970s teachers could write 'Hopeless!' (geography) and 'Very poor!' (physics) and no one turned a hair, whereas I'll be writing 350 to 400 word reports on Year 13, disguising my true feelings throughout? (Not about you, Rebekah.)

Tuesday 30 January

Saw Adrian walking into school from the car park, wearing a tweed cap. Looks incongruous with his sober grey suit.

'Have you noticed the cap?' I said to Jim when the department meeting was over at lunchtime and he and I were left in the office.

'Must be missing the thick and luxurious warmth of his comb-over,' he said while ripping open a KitKat.

'Maybe he regrets shaving it all off. It'll be a wig next,' I said.

If so, Jim wants it to be a giant ginger wig, so we can see Adrian coming in corridors before he sees us.

'My mum had wigs,' I said, although I hadn't planned to.

'Wigs plural? Why?'

I told him she'd had three polystyrene heads.

'Your mother did? What?'

'Lined up on the dressing table, to display the wigs,' I said. 'Large white heads, like ghost heads. One wig black and curly. One red. One brunette.'

'Was she an actor?'

I said she wasn't.

He waited.

'Not actor. Alcoholic. Her hair fell out in clumps. I think it's quite common.'

'Right,' he said. He snapped another finger from the KitKat. 'I did not expect you to say that.'

Nor had I.

I've given Year 13 their drafts back for further work, but the coursework lessons are impossible. Conor has still only written three half-hearted paragraphs. Rebekah, at the other end of the spectrum, has created a thing of beauty. In between are all the others. One-size-fits-all lesson plans are not working, in the same way one-size-fits-all women's tights never have.

Year 11 parents' evening. Missed the bus, so walked home via the chip shop, binning the paper before I got home.

Spouse had cooked tuna pasta with garlic bread. 'I knew you'd be starving,' he said, giving me a kiss.

Am 95 per cent carbohydrate as I write this.

Wednesday 31 January

A miracle! Bathroom Scales say I've stayed the same weight. Stepped off quickly while the going was good. Then, in case they were wrong and I'd actually lost a pound, stepped on more gently. One pound on. Jumped off. Took off glasses. Climbed back on. Still one pound on.

'You must need new batteries,' I said to Bathroom Scales.

Dedicated free periods to progress on *Beauchamp Matters*, despite a desk piled with marking and planning that also matters.

Too many things matter. No wonder I love Baileys.

Although, obviously, my faith is also an enormous source of comfort.

Year 12 now studying World Englishes. Taught them about Chinese English and Japanese English while trying not to sound like a racist. If Ofsted pitch up in the next few days, I'll have to dust off a lesson on the history of dictionaries.

At least they're giving in homework more often, apart from a couple of die-hards whose names I tapped into SIMS. Again.

Year 13 have reached the part where the father in *The Road* coughs uncontrollably, clearly sick. One of the girls slapped her book down and said, 'He's going to die, isn't he? I am not reading another word, Miss, until you tell me there's a happy ending.'

'Er – define "happy",' I said, cautious.

Rebekah looked contemptuous of happy endings, but she probably reads the entire Booker Prize longlist.

Matt is back, a touch subdued.

People at Bible study very solicitous, asking in gentle voices how work was. Spouse said on the way home, 'Did something happen last week when I wasn't there?'

Thursday 1 February

Bahlul looked sickly green this morning. Jim asked whether he'd made himself ill by marking three books.

Colin's staid PowerPoint offering about bullying might have induced vegetative states in Year 11 today, so I'd replaced it. Told them to imagine they were my Year 12 English Language class. 'We'll analyse examples of language used to bully others, in real talk and on social media. It will make you think about your own language use.'

Showed a clip from *EastEnders*, a tense political interview and some vicious tweets aimed at J. K. Rowling. At the end, one girl stayed behind to ask about English Language A level. Talked her through details.

'Would you definitely be one of my teachers?' she said.

Wasn't sure whether she meant she hoped I would be, or rather that I wouldn't.

Not that I'm insecure.

But her interest buoyed me up, so I began my Year 11 English lesson revising two war poems and feeling chipper. Soon brought down by three sullen boys who'd brought their own private war to the lesson. The sniping and veiled threats rumbled on right up to the bell.

Kept the boys in my classroom during break, sat in three corners of the room. I had no access to coffee. No biscuits or cake.

Camilla came in. Could I cover poorly Bahlul's Year 11s in my free period? Please? He'd gone home. I focused really really hard at her mug of coffee, but she didn't get the hint.

Spouse has just said, 'You didn't promise you'd be teaching that girl, did you? What if you're part-time next year with less classes?'

'Fewer,' I said.

Friday 2 February

Bahlul admitted today that an out-of-date pasty from the back of his fridge had caused yesterday's sickness.

I said, 'You mean I had to teach your Year 11s because you gorged yourself on a mouldy pie?'

'I owe you, honest.'

Persuaded him to be profiled by Noora and Betsy for *Beauchamp Matters*.

Then, when George came into the computer room during Journos to collect a broken chair, I thought, *Why only teachers?* Asked him if he'd agree to be interviewed.

'Who by?' He nodded towards where Samuel was peering up at a computer screen. 'This one here? Shrunk in the wash, has he?'

I suspect George has missed some staff training.

Samuel not a bit insulted. He and Aleesha are interviewing George Monday lunchtime.

Leon in Year 8 is bringing the *Frankenstein* novel from home for Friday's reading lessons, but every few minutes he needs definitions of nineteenth-century vocabulary, such as 'hitherto' and 'suppliant'. Handed him a giant dictionary. But at this rate he'll finish the novel by 2023.

Spouse and I went to Leamington for pizza. He wanted to power walk it. I wanted to power bus it. I asked why he couldn't take a break from training for the Olympics and travel by bus to eat his own body weight in bread dough like normal people do on Fridays.

We compromised. Walked it there, but minus the power, and bussed it back.

Monday 5 February

Forgot Year 13 reports until the early hours of Sunday. Sat up in a sweat at 3 a.m., couldn't drift back to sleep, and had to miss church to write them.

Just after Spouse came back, the phone rang. He picked it up. It was Son, asking if we fancied a roast pork dinner. He was serving up in half an hour.

Spouse's eyes said, 'Please don't make me say no to this and eat scrambled egg.'

Abandoned report-writing and we legged it to Son's house.

'Glad you could make it,' DIL said as we crunched on salty crackling and I cut up Grandgirl's pork for her.

'I wanted to be here,' I said, in case they all doubted me.

Ate my meal, trying not to think of all the medical secretaries in the world looking forward to their post-lunch naps and a classic black-and-white movie.

Pressed Save on the last report at 11 p.m.

Today, used my free period to copy and paste the reports into SIMS.

Redesigned Year 11's seating plan to split up the three still-sniping boys permanently. But, I realized too late, this meant two other tricky ones, Jake and Ed, ended up next to each other. 'Do you know what you've done, Miss?' someone asked. The others laughed.

Tried to look unfazed.

Ten minutes into the lesson, my mistake was confirmed and I paid for it with half a lunch break in Jake and Ed's company.

Jim popped his head round my classroom door to announce, 'Pudding is treacle tart.' Then he noticed the boys, and perhaps the way my face fell like a stone. 'Shall I bring you some?'

Angels come in all shapes and sizes.

Even atheist-shape.

Tuesday 6 February

'That is a *corker*,' Mirror said this morning.

'All right, all right, don't hold back.' Pasted my chin's new incandescent spot with the pound-a-dab cream, giving it one more chance to impress.

Dared not tempt Bathroom Scales. Jim had persuaded the catering assistant yesterday I was in great need, so the slice of treacle tart overhung the plate.

Sally, with the help of Samuel and James, has produced a poster about the mini-saga competition. It's all over school. Deadline for entries: end of March, before we break up for Easter. 'We could get hundreds,' I said to Sally, in the office. 'I hope you're prepared.'

She said the word 'mini' was keeping her positive. That reminded me. I told her what George had said about Samuel and she splurted coffee all over her keyboard.

Camilla let Jim do the Top Tips today. He showed us 'Five ways to teach poetry without boring the pants off them'. One was to persuade talented artists in the class to sketch images from poems on the whiteboard. The class guesses which quotation they have in mind. 'It's like poetry Pictionary,' he said. His other four tips were equally creative and made us all feel like beginners.

Bahlul, Sally and I gave Jim an exuberant round of applause until we faltered, realizing we'd never clapped Camilla.

Rebekah has given in her completed coursework early. Sent her to the library to prepare a presentation on dystopian settings. She's delivering it to the class next Wednesday.

Must prepare some intelligent-sounding questions.

Started Year 8 reports tonight. They're due in on Friday. Managed three and a quarter out of twenty-eight.

Spot still raging. Me and pound-a-dab cream are history.

Wednesday 7 February

Overnight toothpaste treatment not a miracle cure, but the spot is only mildly furious today.

And only 0.4 pence a dab.

My two fast-food debate girls spoke to me in registration. Could I check their draft? Between them they've written 1,700 words.

'I think I asked for seven hundred, though,' I said. 'Three hundred and fifty each side of the debate.'

They exchanged panicked looks. They'd already spent hours cutting it from 2,500. One had earned a detention for giving in food tech homework late.

Added the editing job to my list and emailed her food tech teacher to abase myself.

Year 13s explored the theme of memory in their double lesson, analysing McCarthy's use of flashbacks to life before the apocalypse. 'Surely happy memories make their current situation far more tragic?' Conor said in a rare contribution of insight. His cheeks pinked up.

Matt nudged him. 'Steady on. Do you want to, like, stay friends or not?'

'I'd cut your losses, Conor,' Rebekah said.

During a side-track discussion on religious imagery in the novel, Rebekah mentioned that she wants to move church. She says her parents' church is too traditional.

I thought, *What if she comes to my church? And sees me leading worship and playing poor guitar and screeching at the high notes?*

She must be stopped.

When Macbeth realizes he's entertaining thoughts of regicide, he says he feels 'my seated heart knock at my ribs'.

You and me both, Mac.

Went to Bible study carrying a notebook and shamefacedness. Only allowed myself one cookie.

Thursday 8 February

Today's PHSE: What makes someone a bully? Colin's PowerPoint – unusually helpful – explored research into the motivations of bullies, suggesting that the majority have been mistreated themselves.

Felt like two people during the lesson. Person One: adult teacher, dispassionate, objective, advisory, logical, moral. Person Two: confused teenager, conflicted, illogical, with a cruel streak and a need to control.

Did they sense Person Two? One boy questioned my sympathetic stance for bullies. 'I have an even rubbisher home life than some bullies, Miss,' he said, 'but I don't use it as an excuse.'

Like a coward, fobbed him off with a reminder about how to form comparative adjectives.

Not just 'like' a coward.

Year 8 are on Act 3 of *Frankenstein*. The monster has killed Victor Frankenstein's little brother William. Picked a minuscule child to be the corpse of William, carried in by the priest, a much larger and stronger pupil. Kept the reasons for my selections in my own head in a way George wouldn't have.

Leon is bitter that Pullman hasn't included a strangling scene. 'I don't actually get to kill William?' he complained. 'Just a scuffle with Frankenstein?'

'This is an adaptation for schools, Leon,' I said. 'You can't have too much gore and bloodshed.'

'Er – the body parts sewn together?' he said, his arms akimbo.

Lynne thought he had a point.

Zak had hollow places under his eyes in the Year 7 reading lesson. He is like a faded version of himself.

Tonight, I predict little sleep for myself either. My mind, as Macbeth also said, is full of scorpions. My stomach is full of sausage and chips and half a bottle of red wine, consumed after writing more Year 8 reports. But I fear the scorpions have the edge.

Friday 9 February

The scorpions won until 3. When I reached the bathroom this morning and looked at Mirror I flinched. Mirror stayed eerily quiet.

Bathroom Scales, however, had plenty to say. Nothing I wanted to hear. Skipped breakfast and snapped at Spouse when he offered toast. Apologized by text when I was on the bus. But wasn't the damage already done?

Jim's Year 9s are learning how to structure a story. Am using minisagas to teach them, hoping for competition entries.

Break duty was again coffee-less and cake-less. Sally had detainees and couldn't deliveroo. I was super-harsh on the pupils eating illegally in corridors, nibbling warm, sweet cookies as blatantly as anything, in front of my face, my hungry face, my carb-starved face, my snack-free face. A Year 9 boy dropped crumbs on the corridor carpet, so I pulled him aside. 'Would you do that at home?' I asked, pointing to the crumbs.

'Probably,' he said.

I sent his laughing friends away and made him stand with me for five minutes while I lectured on responsibility and respect. He slid the cookie into his pocket while I ranted. 'I'll eat that in maths,' he said.

The Journos are flagging. (Not you, Samuel and James.) I keep lobbing their drafts back at them for improvements. I try to lob kindly, but . . .

'Does this happen with proper magazines?' they asked.

'This *is* a proper magazine,' I told them. 'That's why it's happening.'

Camilla seemed odd this afternoon. I had to repeat something three times before she answered me.

Stayed after school until 7 p.m. finishing Year 8 reports. Three hours past the deadline.

It's early February. By rights, we're due some snow days. A heavy fall on Sunday night and the 'School Closed' text early Monday morning – it's not much to ask.

Monday 12 February

Went to Pizza Express Saturday lunchtime to celebrate Grandgirl's fourth birthday.

'You look tired,' DIL observed with her eagle-eye as we settled and browsed menus.

'I set the alarm for 6. The M word. Don't say it aloud.'

Got involved in a who-feels-most-guilty? conversation. She felt they should have booked for the evening instead to give me the day to work. I felt bad for mentioning it.

Texted Sally later: 'Say it's not just me.'

She texted back: 'Am away with friends. Have brought three sets of marking, my Year 8 reports and a toothbrush. They are horrified.'

Camilla back on form this morning. Her greeting to us all was a reminder about half-term grades.

'That's why I've been marking all weekend,' I said, 'so I've got grades to submit.' Sensed the others going still. Felt suddenly reckless. 'Sorry to sound bitter, Camilla. But sometimes I want a life.'

I could have reached out and pricked myself on her. She said, 'We're all in the same boat,' and pointed to her desk, piled high with books and papers.

'But it's not normal, is it?' I said. 'Knowing they were all in the same boat didn't help those on the *Titanic*.'

Email from Marion Coles asking me to keep to report deadlines. But she added a winky face next to her sign-off.

Tuesday 13 February

Plucked out a long hair growing on my left cheek.

'Why didn't you tell me yesterday?' I said to Mirror. 'It can't have grown that much in one night. I'm a freak.'

'You do dramatize,' Mirror said.

'Dramatize? Dramatize?' I said. 'So would you if you sprouted in the night like some monster triffid. Next, I'll poke Spouse out of the bed with my facial hair and find him on the floor in the morning. I am *not* dramatizing.'

In briefing, Adrian announced that Smuts and heads of department would engage in an official fortnight of espionage and intelligence-gathering to begin after half-term, only he termed it 'learning walks'.

Jim, who knows his union stuff, said, 'Are these formal observations?'

Adrian did the head-smoothing thing. 'Staff will be in the classroom no longer than five minutes, looking at pupils' work.'

I heard Bahlul, next to me, die a little inside.

Year 7 are excited about the mini-saga competition. 'I've told them you can't wait to receive their entries,' I said to Sally, who said it would be a career highlight.

Zak has been to see his mum again, he says. She's back home. He clarified. 'Her home, I mean.' He says she calls going to hospital 'being dried out'.

Being dried out. That's exactly how Mum used to put it. And when I asked her, 'Like grapes are to make raisins?' she said it was something like that. I understand better now. But naivety is more comfortable.

Camilla has asked to see Year 13's coursework pieces. She's keeping an eye on standards, she says.

Come and watch me floss my teeth, why don't you?

Year 12 parents' evening. Camilla and I talked to parents together. Correction: Camilla talked to parents. I slipped in a word or two when she was busy breathing in.

Wednesday 14 February

Spouse still asleep when I woke up today. He'd left a Valentine's card and vase of carnations by the kettle.

Oops.

Best Year 13 lesson ever. Shame I wasn't teaching it. Rebekah's presentation on dystopian settings had it all. Video clips, pictures, group exercises, a mini-quiz, impeccably produced handouts for the class. I'd planned my intelligent questions, but she answered them all in the presentation.

Her delivery style is a touch nursery school teacher, as though any second she'd say 'Why didn't you go at break?' But the others sat dazed, as though she were the Hanging Gardens of Babylon.

She's said nothing else about a new church. Clearly, she doesn't want to talk about it, and it wouldn't be right of me to force the issue.

Detoured to shops on way back from school and bought Spouse a card, two bottles of Rioja, a giant box of Maltesers, a candle, two rump steaks and some chocolate eclairs. Cooked the steak with a wine and cream sauce and brought him his slippers.

I think we're about even. Especially as I gave him the bigger eclair.

We'd sliced into the steaks when we remembered Bible study. They were launching a series on Lent as today was Ash Wednesday.

Started grade reports at 9. Began enthusiastically, inputting Year 7's and Year 8's. By the time I got to Year 11's at 10.30, would have swapped grade reports for a barbed-wire flogging.

Thursday 15 February

Sally has twenty mini-sagas from my Year 9s and Year 7s in her inbox and the same number from other pupils elsewhere. 'Listen to this from one of your Year 9s.' She read it to me. 'Isn't that brilliant?'

'Hold on. Type the first sentence into Auntie Google,' I said.

Thought so. It was one I'd used in the Year 9 lesson as a model. Asked Sally to forward the email to me.

She said, 'Tell her all she had to do was write fifty words from her own brain cells. We're not asking for Dostoevsky here.'

Said I would quote her exactly.

Sent the Year 9 a note via her tutor to come to the English office at break. She pitched up, red-faced. Sally was in there too.

'You probably know why you're here,' I began.

She bit her lip. 'Is it because I wrote a note to Kelly in your last lesson saying I was really bored?'

Er . . .

Sally projectile-guffawed and hurried out, pleading photocopying.

'We could hear you laughing as you went down the stairs,' I told her later. 'Thanks for your unwavering support.'

For PHSE, Colin provided imaginary case studies of bullied pupils. I split the class into fours, appointing each pupil in the group either a headteacher, form tutor, school council member or parent. 'Come to an agreement', I said, 'about what action should or shouldn't be taken.'

'Shouldn't there be a bullied child and a bully in each group too?' someone asked.

Why hadn't I thought of that?

'I have a better idea,' I said. 'Let's put a bullied child and a bully in each group.'

Uneven numbers meant I had to play a bully. It wasn't easy.

Spouse has discovered meditations that involve repeating phrases aloud. Could hear him from the study as I marked essays tonight. It's a bit Buddhist, isn't it?

Asked him to close the door to the lounge, then felt mean.

Friday 16 February

Went to work early to finish grade reports. Found Sally in the office, doing the same. She'd bought an extra cinnamon pastry. 'I knew you'd be here,' she said.

The pastry was still warm.

We tapped into our laptops companionably until Bahlul arrived and asked us what we were typing.

'Grade reports,' Sally said. 'Camilla did remind us all on Monday.'

He had to lean against the door jamb.

At break duty, while I ate my cake, a Year 7 boy was sick in the corridor, retching up his cooked breakfast. Not much puts me off carrot cake, but . . .

His performance drew a keen crowd.

Asked if someone could run to Reception for a cleaner or care-taker. The crowd herded down the corridor. 'I said "some*one*",' I shouted.

Recruited a passing Year 11 to take the khaki-faced vomiter to the sickroom before he brought up a third sausage.

George arrived with a bucket. The crowd returned to watch him clear up.

'Go. Away,' I said. 'This is not Netflix.'

They drifted off.

The bell rang for lessons. 'Sorry, George,' I said. 'I have to go and teach Year 12 about lingua francas.'

He said rather me than him.

Took chocolate biscuits for the Journos at lunchtime to keep their spirits up while I critiqued their spelling, punctuation, grammar, structure and vocabulary.

They promised to work on articles over half-term.

'You promised the same at Christmas,' I said, sceptical.

They promised again.

Submitted grade reports five minutes before deadline.

Camilla says she has 'some misgivings about the Year 13 course-work, which we can discuss after half-term'.

Happy holidays to you too, Camilla.

Second half of spring term

Monday 26 February

Alarm rang at 6. Put one tentative foot out of the duvet and snatched it back. We'd forgotten to re-adjust the heating timer again. Spouse still snoring.

Shivered in the shower and dressed in the dark. Comforted myself by comparing my lot to people in Siberia and Antarctica, and anyone trapped for weeks in a cold store.

Bathroom Scales regretted to inform me that half-term has resulted in another pound gain. This I blame on all the times I went for a brisk walk but only in my head.

Sally has been skiing and showed me pictures.

'Where's Archie?' I said.

'Oh, I went with friends,' she said. 'Archie's not really into skiing.'

Zak's mum is back in hospital. She fell while walking to the corner shop in dressing gown and slippers. 'She'd run out of milk,' he said.

I remember my mum saying, 'I've run out of fags.' But fags in a carrier bag didn't clink that way – not that I ever dared to say it.

Good Year 7 lesson, though, creating fictional characters. That is, until a boy leaned back too far on his chair. It slid from under him. He yelped in pain and lay crying. Everyone stood to gawp. Then half a class of Year 8s, left unsupervised next door while Bahlul fetched a forgotten book, stampeded in to see the action.

That's when Camilla arrived for a learning walk.

Tuesday 27 February

Year 7 on geography trip so no Period 2 lesson. Hid in library behind Senior Fiction.

Camilla, a sniffer dog in a previous life, found me. She wanted to talk about (a) why Year 7 lessons should not resemble Bedlam and (b) Year 13 coursework.

She thinks my coursework marking is too generous. (Not you, Rebekah.)

She thinks five out of seven pupils need to redraft.

She thinks I should help them redraft.

'But I've given so much support already,' I said. 'More than the board officially recommends. I want them to focus on the exam texts now.'

By lunchtime, though, she had gone off sick and we had no departmental meeting. Maybe looking at Conor's coursework murdered her immune system.

After Year 13's lesson on *The Road*, kept the Coursework Five behind and explained that Miss Stent felt they could do better. Gave them a new deadline for Tuesday 13 March.

'But you'd already, like, decided on marks,' Matt said.

Chorus: 'Yeah!'

'Nothing's set in stone. You can all improve,' I said.

'Will you give us help?'

Checked the door, in case Camilla had experienced a miracle healing. 'As well as the help already given? If I help you any more, the Samaritans will headhunt me.'

They are properly dischuffed.

Also, Conor has sold his coursework texts on ebay.

Wednesday 28 February

I have three spots in a row on my left cheek, like the dot-dot-dot ellipsis that creates tension in a story.

'If you must suffer menopausal spots,' Mirror said, 'isn't it a comfort when they resemble a linguistic feature?'

My form thinks life is unfair. Schools are closed all over the UK because of snow disruption, but ours has been spared.

Year 12 are still studying the use of English in the wider world. I started the lesson by asking, 'Who knows what a pidgin is?'

Only the Privates knew I wasn't talking about bird life. The rest were baffled as to why I'd ask. One embarked on a full description, except that when she impersonated the noise they make, she'd been describing a seagull.

They wrote down a definition: 'A form of contact language acting as a lingua franca between people who don't share a common language.'

Matt said he could do with a pidgin in his business studies lessons because the class didn't understand a word Mr Short said, and neither did Mr Short understand the pupils.

Year 13's double lesson was awkward. The Coursework Five were mutinous and contributed nothing. I joked, 'We're at the end of *The Road*,' but only Rebekah smiled.

Spouse and I arrived at Bible study. They said they'd missed us last week. I described our Valentine's Day evening. Steak. Cream sauce. Candles. Chocolate eclairs. A glass of wine.

Then I remembered it had been Ash Wednesday.

They were gracious about it.

Spouse has just said as he nestled under the duvet, 'You failed to mention that you forgot Valentine's Day and had to dash to the shops after school. I'm sure you meant to.'

Told him to shush or I'd shine my mini-light straight in his eyes.

Thursday 1 March

Have slipped into a pattern: am spending two hours asleep, two hours awake.

Jim said, 'It's a useful skill should you ever sail the Atlantic single-handedly.'

Told him I'd bear it in mind.

Bore it in mind through another of Adrian's Year 11 assembly lectures, this one a sop to World Book Day. He talked about his favourite childhood books. Made them sound as exciting as a trip to the shops to buy curtain rings.

But someone's tipped him off about not susurrating. He kept the microphone well away from his mouth. Not far enough away, unfortunately.

Also bore it in mind through my Year 11 lesson in which four pupils earned themselves detentions.

Bore it in mind during the detentions while they filled in my forms with faces like gathering storms.

Last session on bullying in PHSE. Can't say I'm upset. I've felt like a fraud.

Year 7 celebrated World Book Day by coming to school dressed as fictional characters: Harry Potters, Matildas, Paddington Bears, the Wimpy Kids. By Period 5, the costumes were less convincing. I offended a Where's Wally by calling him Burglar Bill. He'd lost his woolly hat and said his granny's round glasses had made his eyes go weird so he'd taken them off.

Year 8 parents' evening after school. Missed the bus back. Comforted myself with a giant steaming cone of fat, salty chips while I trudged home. Kept my hood up in case anyone I know drove past.

I feel a rhyming couplet coming on.

They came to detention and filled in my forms
With faces upon them like gathering storms

Have read it to Spouse. He's unimpressed. He was just dropping off.

Why don't I just tell the truth to, say, Sally?

Sally, I bullied smaller children at secondary school when I was in the fourth and fifth year. I hung around in the girls' toilets with friends equally as mean. We tormented the first-years, rattling cubicle doors, laughing at them, blowing smoke in their faces.

Writing it down makes my stomach flip. To say it aloud? To someone as sweet as Sally?

No.

Friday 2 March

Would have drowned last night had I been sailing the Atlantic single-handedly as I slept for six hours (anaesthetized by chips), but woke at 5 a.m. Odd dream, though, in which Rebekah came to church with Camilla and they both heckled while I sang Elvis numbers, getting the words wrong.

Bathroom Scales very kind today, considering the chips. Have lost the pound I'd put on.

'She's wearing lighter pyjamas, though,' Mirror said.

'*She* is present,' I said.

Took cake to Journos. Most worked hard over half-term and my inbox contains the evidence. Only Lukas had done nothing. 'Can I still have cake for looking like I do?' he said.

I *think* he was joking.

Gave him a small slice and made him promise to speed up with the sports reports. He enjoyed the irony, and something's better than nothing.

Noora has taken charge of the bullying article. She told me she'd arrived at Beauchamp in Year 9 after being bullied at a previous school. She has plenty of ideas about what schools should do to help.

I advised her on its structure and corrected some spellings.

'I'm still having counselling, Miss,' she said. 'It made me scared to go outdoors.'

Year 8 Leon is still battling with *Frankenstein.* I noticed the girl beside him reading an abridged version of *Jane Eyre.* 'It was in the school library,' she said. 'I think there's a series.'

Sent Leon with Lynne to talk to the librarian. He returned with an abridged *Frankenstein* and a grin like a champion.

Monday 5 March

Spouse has ratcheted the power walking up a notch. Yesterday he went twice: once before church and once after lunch while I marked.

'I feel like a blobfish by comparison,' I said, when he returned at 3, his face glowing. 'Or a sloth. A sloth who marks, reads and writes. Parked in a chair. Sedentary. Or s*edent*ary. However you're supposed to say it. How *are* you supposed to say it? Why don't I know?'

He slipped off his trainers. 'You sound fed up. You should have come. The sun's doing its best out there.'

Said I might go for a stroll, once I'd finished a pile of Year 8 books. But by then dusk was falling. And Spouse had opened some red wine.

'I'll just have to power drink instead,' I said.

'No Sunday evening planning?'

I said Sunday evening planning had turned into Monday morning free period planning.

Bad decision. The Monday morning free got swallowed up. Camilla asked me to cover a lesson for Sally, who had a medical appointment. Bye bye, planning. Hello, winging it.

Winging it isn't conducive to orderly lessons. When Colin turned up for a learning walk during my Year 11 double, I'd just written 'Danger Zone' on the board and was adding three names underneath as a warning.

Still, they quietened when Colin appeared. He flicked through their books and declared himself taken with their writing about 'The Charge of the Light Brigade'. He told them, maintaining eye contact with the walls only, that he'd studied it at school too. 'Half a league, half a league,' he chanted, bobbing up and down, and then again, 'Half a league, half a league.' The pupils watched him, enthralled, in the same way people watch *Embarrassing Bodies*.

Saw Sally after school and said I hoped her doctor's appointment had gone well. She said she hadn't been at the doctor's. 'Archie and I were seeing our bank manager. We're in it up to our necks.'

Tuesday 6 March

Leon was happy today to find out that Pullman has the monster strangling Frankenstein's cousin Elizabeth on stage. He looked so keen that the small Year 8 girl I have/had playing Elizabeth stepped back as he approached.

'Don't put your hands on her neck,' I said, 'in case anyone comes in for a learning walk.'

'And in case he hurts her,' Lynne said.

'And in case you hurt her,' I said.

Taught Year 12 about Schneider's dynamic model and how it explains the way English spreads throughout a new territory. Gus Private had already read the chapter and tossed around the terminology – exonormative stabilization, nativization, endonormative stabilization, differentiation – as though he's been speaking fluent Linguistic since his father's sperm hit his mother's ovum. The other Year 12 boys hate him for it. At least the girl Privates tend not to flaunt their knowledge like an expensive watch.

Gus had to leave early for a music lesson. Relief! The atmosphere had been tight with things left unsaid.

Not for long. 'He makes me want to deck him,' declared one of the boys, loudly enough for Gus to hear before he shut the door.

There was a pause.

'I hope that's not a serious threat,' I said. 'I'd have to report it.'

'I wouldn't waste my fist,' he said.

I couldn't work out whether that improved the situation or not.

'Anyway,' I said. 'Let's move on. Did anyone notice what happened there, linguistically?'

'I said I wanted to deck Gus,' said the boy.

'I mean, the switch from Gus's specialist lexical discourse to your colloquial expression.'

He stared at me as though I'd spoken in Punjabi.

Year 13 parents' evening. Again, seeing parents alongside Camilla. Rebekah's parents were delightful as usual. Dad looks like Charles Dickens. Mum diminutive with enormous glasses. Both very proud of their daughter.

After them, Conor and his dad approached. 'Your faces actually collapsed when you saw us,' Conor said to me and Camilla as they sat down.

Camilla was not happy that I laughed.

Wednesday 7 March

Turned my alarm off at 6, then put my head back on the pillow.

Soon, I was on a ship, being rocked backwards and forwards. 'Wake up. It's ten past seven,' said Spouse, shaking my shoulders.

In the bathroom, Mirror said, 'Isn't your hair due for a wash?'

I said, 'Aren't you due for a lesson in sensitivity?'

Hurtled through the office door five minutes into registration, when I should have been with my Year 11 form.

Camilla was there, taking a handful of tablets. She turned away when I came in. Only caught a glance before grabbing my planner, but – three, four pills?

Several Year 12s missing because of university open days, so the atmosphere was less tense. Gus Private unusually quiet.

The Head of Sixth Form has emailed to say we should check registers carefully. Some Year 12s are claiming to attend open days but are at home playing Fortnite or doing a shift at Boots.

Year 13 wrote a practice comparison essay on Atwood and McCarthy. 'You can start,' I said from my Jim-position behind them.

Conor put a copy of each novel on his desk.

Rebekah reached over and dropped them back in his bag. 'It's a closed-book exam. Honestly, how many *times*?'

'Do we need an introduction?' one of the girls asked.

Rebekah said, 'Of *course*.'

The girl said, 'OK. Thanks, Rebekah.'

Cleared my throat to remind them I was there and indispensable.

Later, when I took the essays in, the Coursework Five asked to speak to me.

Uh oh.

They'd spoken to Miss Stent. She'd suggested they ask me politely for an after-school tutorial. Or two.

Oh, had she now?

Missed Bible study. Told Spouse I'd be marking, but also that I needed the evening to seethe, and at Bible study I'd run the risk of having to stop.

Assessed all the Year 13 practice essays as well as some Year 7 books. Seething definitely speeds up the marking.

Thursday 8 March

The new PHSE subject is exercise. Today, Colin's dry-as-a-board PowerPoint, which I hadn't had time to adapt, was about the link between lack of exercise and different diseases such as dementia or osteoporosis. A bit depressing, isn't it, for a class of fifteen-year-olds? Like saying, 'Today's special guest is the Grim Reaper, here to chat to you about the inevitability of death.'

Next week's lesson is about different kinds of exercise. Somehow I know, deep in my soul, that I'll be forced to sing the praises of power walking. But has there been one day in my teaching career when I haven't felt like a hypocrite?

What's the option? The truth?

'My husband goes power walking to keep fit, but if he asks me to go, I hide under the table and eat Snickers bars.'

'I tell you not to obsess about your appearance, but each morning I critique myself in front of a malicious mirror.'

'I'm telling you not to bully others, but there's a mean streak in me I'm worried hasn't disappeared.'

Hey, where did that come from? Am I? Worried it hasn't disappeared?

Spouse has just asked while getting into bed, 'How's the diary going? Are you enjoying writing it?'

Told him it was really fun, thanks.

Oh, and we had the second twilight teacher training session of the year after school today. It was about cognitive skills, particularly memory.

Friday 9 March

I've a spot on my neck, under my left ear. It's fierce-red and thrumming like an engine. All day, wore a pink woolly scarf so big I could unravel it and make seventeen cardigans.

If I could knit.

Three pupils asked if I had a cold. One of Jim's Year 9 girls on the front row asked if it was a goitre.

'How do you know about goitres?' I said.

'My granddad's got one,' she said. 'It looks like a hill on his neck.'

I asked if he was having it removed.

'They'll try. When are you having yours done?'

'I haven't got a goitre!' I said.

She looked dubious. 'There's no shame in admitting it.'

Sally brought coffee and chocolate cake to break duty. 'What's with the pink sheep round your neck? Are you poorly?'

I told her the truth about the spot. It was worth a go.

'No one notices these things,' she said. 'I've told you.'

I lifted the scarf.

She drew in a breath. '*Oof.*'

'See?'

'Only because you drew attention to it.'

I'm right, then. If I told her more truths, she might *oof* about those too.

Tried to turn the heating down in the computer room during Journos, but they complained.

'I'm roasting,' I said.

'But Miss, you're wearing a mahoosive scarf,' Aleesha said.

Lukas said he thought the scarf was wearing Miss.

Stripped off my jacket and cardigan, leaving myself in a cotton top and a ton of pink wool. Fanned my face with a sheaf of papers, trying to ignore the students' puzzled glances.

Sent them off five minutes early when I started feeling light-headed.

Lynne was away today. I sat at the back of the Year 8 reading lesson so they couldn't stare at me.

Got home and unravelled myself. The spot is angrier and looks infected. I think I may have fermented it.

Monday 12 March

Went shopping on Saturday and found a purple polo neck jumper in Cats Protection. I owned a similar one in 1976.

Wore it on Sunday while I led worship. Could feel the spot pulsating away underneath, as though threatening to appear over the rim of the polo neck like a prisoner scaling a fence.

That would have livened up the worship time. Who needs the Pentecostals?

Son and family came for Sunday lunch as it was Son's birthday weekend. He and DIL sneaked off to Leamington for coffee while we entertained the Littluns. They didn't find my marking and Grandpa's dozing that entertaining, so we played Uno and watched *Horrid Henry* instead.

At bedtime yesterday, Pompeiied the spot with half a tube of toothpaste, and overnight it had faded to annoyed.

Tried to cheer myself up this morning by getting on Bathroom Scales. Hoped I'd lost weight. But I didn't like the way the numbers were going, so leapt off again.

Mirror said, 'She can move fast when it matters.'

Year 11 English class produced more work for me today by writing a practice English Language paper. And they've done homework essays on poetry.

'Keep it up,' I said. 'You have exactly eight weeks until your first exam. Not that I'm trying to scare you.'

'You are totally trying to scare us,' one girl complained. 'At least be honest.'

At least be honest. Ha!

Tuesday 13 March

The spot now looks like a love bite. Wore the polo neck to school. My life is complicated enough.

Camilla late in today. She looks pallid in the way Year 11 girls do when they haven't eaten breakfast.

She appeared at the door during my Year 7 lesson, beckoning.

'Carry on inventing your fantasy protagonist,' I said to the class. 'I'll be back in a second.'

Lynne waved to say, *I'll watch them.*

I hadn't even reached the door when . . .

Pupil 1: 'Miss, wait. What's a –'

'It's on the board and I've explained it twice,' I said.

Pupil 2: 'Miss, I don't have my book. It's on your desk. You were marking it.'

Dashed back to the desk, then started for the door again.

Pupil 3: 'Miss, before you go, do you have a spare pen? Mine's run out.'

Back to the desk again.

Lynne said, 'Go, quick. I have a pen.'

Camilla said in the corridor, 'Hope I haven't interrupted anything.'

No, no, of course not. We were just chillin', Camilla, and I was about to give out the choc ices.

She said, 'I'm busy at break, so thought I'd catch you now – touch base on the Year 13 coursework thing.'

Thing? It wasn't a Thing until she made it a Thing.

And why couldn't she base-touch later, at the department meeting?

Kept my grip on the door handle. I said, 'I've told Year 13 I'll dedicate today's lesson to coursework. But that means sending Rebekah and one other girl to the library to work rather than teaching them, of course.'

She looked untouched.

'Then,' I added, 'I'll see them after school for another hour. That's all I can offer. But I'm not writing their coursework for them.'

'No one's asking you to,' she said, while her eyes asked me to.

Top Tips at lunchtime from Sally about starter activities. Tip-top top tips. She got applause.

There's fright in Bahlul's eyes in case he's asked to top-tip anyone.

Year 13's hour after school became two hours and forty minutes. Spouse's cottage pie had given up hope and lay struggling for breath when I arrived home.

Wednesday 14 March

Sally's had a flurry of new email entries for the mini-saga competition. She looked at her screen. 'Hey, they're all from Bahlul's Year 8s.'

'He doesn't miss a trick,' Jim said. 'Competition entry. Free lesson idea. Free homework. Someone else marks it.'

'It's meant to be their choice whether they enter,' I said.

Bahlul walked into the office.

'Oi, you,' I said. 'Did you press-gang your Year 8s into mini-sagas?'

He looked offended. How could we doubt him? He'd merely given them a choice between writing an essay on the class novel or submitting a mini-saga.

Spent the day in denial about my workload and dedicated both free periods to *Beauchamp Matters*. Transferring articles from email to files. Proofreading. Editing. Sending back material for improvement.

Sports reports are beginning to trickle in, thanks to the Head of Games, a handsome ex-footballer. He told me in the staffroom that he'd try to galvanize Lukas for me and I said, 'I actually want to cuddle you,' then regretted it because it was true.

Gave Year 13 last week's timed essays back. Improvements are happening gradually (you don't need them, Rebekah) and even Matt and Conor's marks are better.

Either that, or marking under the influence of seething swayed my judgement.

Tonight, Spouse met a friend at the pub, so I went to Bible study alone. Everyone has given something up for Lent or taken up something worthy for Lent. Told them I'd given up self-restraint. One or two laughed, presumably to humour me.

I don't suppose even Michael McIntyre gets it right *every* time.

Thursday 15 March

Year 8 have finished *Frankenstein*, so they're studying other examples of Gothic writing. Today we started Edgar Allen Poe's poem 'The Raven'.

'The Raving?' someone said. 'What, like, mad people?'

'Dancing?' someone else suggested.

Goater: 'She said "*raven*". It's a poem about a *raven*.' She's more supercilious than ever.

'What's a raven?' said a boy at the front. 'Never heard of them. Are they extinct?'

Auntie Google images. My saviour.

Leon is now reading the abridged *Jane Eyre* and told me when everyone had left for lunch that he's moving on to *Jekyll and Hyde* next.

'What were you reading before?' I said.

He said he wasn't.

'Leon,' I said. 'Would you like to write something for the new school magazine?'

'Me?'

'I'll help you.'

He shrugged, as if not sure how to react. 'S'pose.'

He's coming to see me tomorrow break, while I'm on duty.

Apparently, what Spouse is doing is speed walking, not power walking. I've told him. I thought he should know.

'Who says?' he said, sleepily.

'Colin's PowerPoint.'

'Who's Colin SpowerPoint?'

Spouse thinks he's so funny.

Friday 16 March

'No scarf this week?' one of Jim's Year 9s asked today. 'Is your goitre better?'

'There *is* no goitre,' I said. 'Can we start the lesson, please?'

Leon drifted along at break, clearly self-conscious to be standing with the duty teacher, as though he'd been naughty. 'Let's dodge into this classroom,' I said. 'I can keep an eye from there.'

A maths question. What's the probability that if a duty teacher leaves the corridor for five minutes, someone will be tripped over by a friend and break a wrist?

Another question. What's the probability that the headmaster will enter the corridor at that point?

Rushed out of the classroom when I heard the yell, with Leon behind me. Found a white-faced Year 7 child holding a strangely angled wrist, his friend beside him wailing, 'It was a joke. Honest!' Adrian stood there, looking panicked.

'I'll go and tell Reception,' I said.

'No, I'll go.' Adrian hurried off.

Once the child had been taken to the sickroom to await an ambulance, I realized Leon was still in the corridor. Then the bell rang for Period 3. I apologized, but he said it had been fun.

Have allocated pairs of Journos to do pupil interviews. Reminded them we only have six weeks left until the magazine goes to print. George and Bahlul's profile interviews are now in my inbox, and Samuel and James hesitantly agreed to see Mr Vinnicombe, who'd emailed me offering himself up.

James is upset about Stephen Hawking's death and has suggested a piece called 'Ten top scientists you should know about'. He's writing fifty words on each.

Betsy asked whether she could write a similar piece about her top ten *Love Island* contestants.

I said no.

'*Similar?*' James was shaking his head.

Samuel touched his arm to comfort him.

Monday 19 March

The Littluns came for another sleepover on Saturday. Son and DIL at a wedding. Weather too cold for parks and walks, so we stayed in and made paper snowflakes, animals out of cereal packets, and some rock cakes that lived up to their name.

'I'll message Mummy and tell her what you've been doing,' I said.

'Send her some pictures,' Grandgirl suggested. 'That's what Daddy does.'

Of course. Send pictures. 'Oops. Just taken a photo of my foot. Hang on.'

She giggled.

Roll up, roll up. Free entertainment. Watch Grandma techno-fail.

Still, was completely spot-free on Sunday, probably because I wasn't leading worship.

Year 8 are loving Poe's raven poem. They're illustrating quotations with dark-coloured pencils Lynne fetched from Art.

Pupil 1: 'Is there any pink?'

Pupil 2: 'No. There's no pink in Gothic.'

Pupil 3: 'Can I do a stick raven? I'm no good at drawing birds.'

Pupil 4: 'I can draw a robin. Can it be a robin?'

I suggested that 'The Robin' didn't have the same Gothic vibe as a name for a poem, but if she wanted to, she could sketch the outline of a robin, then colour it in black.

In the Year 7 lesson, Zak said that his mum had a 'frombosis' from lying down for so long after her fall. Also, his dad has moved away without saying goodbye to either of his children. But he's left Oscar the spaniel, and Zak's foster parents have agreed to let Zak keep him.

Angel Child listens to Zak's updates with wide eyes, as though his world is one she thought only happened in books.

Tuesday 20 March

Forgot to set alarm and woke up late. Managed three sips of tea and one bite of Spouse's toast and marmalade.

In briefing, Adrian spoke darkly about staff duties. 'We are in loco parentis. Any teacher not at their post when there's an incident could get us into serious trouble.' My cheeks burned, although he didn't mention my name. Sally glanced at me with sympathy.

Back in the office, she said, 'It could happen to any of us.' She laid a piece of carrot cake wrapped in a serviette on my desk.

'Hello, breakfast!' I said.

Took the cake with me to nibble while walking to registration, but saw Adrian coming and slid it into my jacket pocket.

Are you sure, Adrian, you're not up for trying a ginger wig?

Year 7 were meant to do a comprehension test today based on an extract from a fantasy novel they'd read for homework. Three had lost the piece of paper with the extract on it. Two were absent, presumed ill. Two had stayed at their dad's/mum's at the weekend and had forgotten to take the homework with them. Four said they hadn't understood it.

Amidst all this, a girl said she felt sick.

Had a conflab with Lynne, with our backs to the class. 'Have you got a Plan B?' she asked.

I could only come up with emigration.

In the end, we played 'literary terms' hangman with a five-minute hiatus when the girl was actually sick, as promised. Lynne grabbed the bin in time, but the girl's fantasy novel extract was splattered.

'You should of lost yours like we did,' a friend advised her.

Made a note to photocopy another fifteen for Friday.

In the last lesson of the day, the Coursework Five submitted their coursework, but even an after-dinner Baileys didn't supply me with the courage to read them.

Spouse hung my jacket up for me this evening. 'What's this in your pocket?' he said, then withdrew his fingers. But not fast enough to avoid getting vanilla-frosted.

Wednesday 21 March

Haven't done any more on my reading diary article. All I have is a draft. Scan-read it again today and realized it's as rough as bricks. It'll have to wait for the Easter holidays.

Camilla asked if I'd decided on final marks for Year 13's coursework. She says Marion is leaning on all departments to get high coursework grades. They're worried the cohort's exam results won't be strong enough to hit our targets.

She seemed desperate today. There was an edge of anxiety to her voice I haven't heard before.

Unless I haven't been listening.

She has prominent cheekbones. I'm sure she's thinner.

Had to SIMS half the Year 12 class today for late homework. Gus doesn't help things. He submits each essay in a postbox-red plastic wallet with a flourish, like a bunch of flowers.

'I don't need the plastic wallet, Gus,' I keep saying. 'A paper clip is fine.'

'I don't want to get my work mixed up with the others,' he said today, fortunately only to me.

Studied religious imagery in *Handmaid* and *The Road* with Year 13. Dangerous territory. I know the others think Rebekah strange and other-worldly with her faultless biblical knowledge and the way she speaks so naturally about church. I should really say something so that she has an ally.

Spouse was late home after seeing a garden, so he fetched fish and chips on the way back from his powerspeed walk, then we rushed to Bible study.

Confessed to the group, 'I have skirted around the mention of church with my Year 13s in case one of them comes along.'

Did I heck.

Looked in Mirror when I got home tonight to examine my own cheekbones.

'Good luck with that,' Mirror said.

Thursday 22 March

Not sleeping. What pattern I'd established has gone. Dabbed the white cream on to the eye bags this morning, but I can't see any difference, except that I have slippy eye bags.

Also, I swear my face is sinking further, like a landslide. I pulled up both jowls with my hands to see what it used to look like.

'A chin!' Mirror said. 'Nostalgia!'

Let the jowls down again. Like dropping bread dough into a mixing bowl.

Bathroom Scales of no help to self-worth. Two pounds on again. 'Will that be the fish and chips?' they said, mildly.

'She didn't eat all the batter, surely,' Mirror said. 'It's the batter that's the killer.'

'She did not eat all the batter,' I said.

'But did she make herself a chip butty?' Mirror said.

'She did not eat all the batter,' I said.

Ditched Colin SpowerPoint – a tedious litany of facts and figures about the benefits of exercise to the internal organs. I saw an article last week on the BBC website about boys over-exercising to look like men on *Love Island*. I showed it to the class.

'Is it true?' I said. 'Tell me.'

Floodgates!

And I've learned the word 'hench', as in 'He's bare hench'. In English, this means 'He's very fit and strong-looking'.

Apparently, bare hench is the pinnacle.

I begged them to stop watching programmes like *Love Island*, but they laughed in my face.

Leon found me in the office at break time and we talked. Result! He'll draft an article over Easter on how abridged books have lured him into reading.

Friday 23 March

Four days to go until Easter holidays.

'Next Friday is Good Friday!' Sally said.

'In more ways than one,' I said, before I could stop myself.

What kind of Christian says things like that? Especially at Lent. (Not you, I bet, Rebekah.)

Jim's Year 9 also had an eye on the calendar. 'This is our last lesson of the term, Miss.'

'And?'

'Can we write more jokes?'

'I'm not doing Easter jokes.'

'We don't mean jokes about Jesus,' they protested. 'Who'd do that?'

Er . . .

'We could do chocolate jokes,' they said. 'And bunny jokes. Maybe we could tell you what sentence structures we're using.'

Blackmail!

We wrote chocolate and bunny jokes and I kept them to their promise. They're accepting subordinate clauses into their lives more willingly than my Year 12s, that's for sure.

Two Year 12s missing today, having claimed university visits. One was telling the truth. The other was in Warwick town centre, having a haircut.

Have sent email to Colin, proposing an assembly about body image for Years 10 and 11. Summarized the 'bare hench' lesson for him. After I pressed Send, I realized that he might ask why I hadn't delivered the 'benefits to body organs' lesson.

He emailed back: 'Your helpful suggestions are much appreciated. I do hope you can catch up on the timetabled lesson soon.'

Samuel and James have interviewed Paul Vinnicombe and written it up, although they seem unsettled by the experience, which took a whole lunch break. Samuel said, 'I don't think pupils listen to Mr Vinnicombe very often. Did you know he used to be a trapeze artist?'

Monday 26 March

Led worship on Sunday while thinking, *How would I feel if Rebekah were in the congregation, watching me choose a G chord every time I need an F?*

But what if she really does need a new, lively church?

Flicked through the Gospels during the sermon. It turns out Jesus did say that anyone who causes children who believe in him to stumble should have a millstone round their necks and be drowned in the depths of the sea.

Was hoping I'd remembered it wrong.

Email from Camilla this morning, reminding me that tomorrow is my Top Tips slot. She sent the email at 5 a.m.

I'd forgotten, so cheerybye, Monday free period.

She peered into my classroom at break while I was supervising a couple of Year 8s I'd kept behind. She looked surprised to see me at the back.

I went to the door. 'My new strategy. Keeps them wondering.'

I'm not even sure she heard. She looked distracted. 'Did you get my message about Top Tips?' she said.

'It's all in hand. Hurrah for frees!'

She looked as though she'd go, but didn't.

After a few seconds, she said, 'While I'm here – er – I wondered – Sally says you're working on an article about children's reading.' She fiddled with a jacket button.

I hadn't thought. But, of course. She was teaching the Year 12s how children learn to read. I asked if she'd like my notes as well as the data. She'd get three lessons out of all the materials.

She looked hunted. Vulnerable. 'I'm so grateful,' she said.

She walked down the corridor and I turned back into the classroom. The Year 8s were putting away their pens. 'Not so fast,' I said. 'Let me check those forms.'

Tuesday 27 March

In case we were looking forward to the Easter holidays, Adrian reminded us in briefing that next term we'd probably be Ofsteded.

Sally said, in the office, 'Well, he can stuff himself. I'm taking *zero* work to Devon.' She asked if I was going anywhere.

Told her I'd probably venture out to Tesco at some point.

Bahlul said he was going to the States for a fortnight. He'd catch up on his marking this week, before he went. Sally, Jim and I turned to look at his desk, crazy with teetering towers of exercise books and piles of handwritten essays.

At lunch, my colleagues listened to my top tips while eating shortbread Sally had baked. I focused on joke writing and its usefulness for teaching metaphor, sentence structure, homophone spellings such as 'bear' and 'bare', characterization and vocabulary.

'That was truly excellent,' Camilla said, when I stopped.

There was a pause. Had we heard right?

'So, do I get a clap?' I said to them, eventually.

Camilla clapped with her fingertips – and was eyeing up the shortbread crumbs on the carpet while she did it – but hey, small mercies.

She also told us she'd postponed a Key Stage 4 work audit until after Easter. There were half-term grades to do first.

'Since when did Camilla postpone things?' Sally said when she'd left.

The Coursework Five wanted to know if I'd read their updated pieces. Not that they've left worrying about their progress until last minute or anything.

Sally dropped me home tonight. I asked her how things were going with Archie.

'That's what Devon's all about,' she said. 'Time to talk. A proper rest – though in the cheapest hotel I could find.'

Wednesday 28 March

Lost a pound, probably because I was delivering top tips while everyone else ate shortbread yesterday. 'Yay!' said Bathroom Scales. 'Well done, you.'

'Well done, her,' said Mirror, but not as kindly.

I leaned nearer to Mirror. 'Another white hair in my eyebrow?' I groaned. 'I am turning into Miss Havisham.'

'Except that she wears a wedding dress,' Mirror said.

Spent my frees on *Beauchamp Matters* again, emailing heads of department to ask for reports of trips or achievements and then the Art department begging for images of pupils' work.

Full complement of Year 12s. Their year head has cracked down on fake uni visits. Jim says Marion says that the Head of Science threatened resignation unless something happened.

'Too right,' Jim said to me. 'Otherwise you're chasing the beggars, catching them up on missed topics, photocopying this, that and the other, so they can lie in bed stuffing nachos.'

Jim says Marion says.

Marion says a lot to Jim.

Spent today's Year 12 lesson on David Crystal's theories. The pupils mostly join in with the response now. I knew I'd beat them down.

Year 13 wrote practice essay paragraphs. They didn't make the usual fuss. I feel almost hopeful.

Not so encouraging was that every time I looked at Rebekah I saw a millstone.

The Coursework Five wanted another update. 'I'll have more time over Easter to peruse them,' I said, 'and chocolate to sustain me.'

'You might need it,' said Conor, soberly. 'I think I've made mine worse.'

Got the giggles in Bible study, seeing humour in a parable everyone else took seriously. One man looked at me the way people look at neglected ponies.

Thursday 29 March

'A half-day!' Bahlul said first thing today. 'We finish at lunch!' He was at his desk, tick-tick-ticking work.

'No we don't,' I said. 'Not at Easter.'

His eyes widened. 'But my flight's at 4 from Birmingham Airport.'

Jim came in. 'What's up?'

Bahlul explained his dilemma.

'Don't you check the school calendar?' Jim said. 'Surely you've had to read out the notices to your Year 10 form?'

Apparently, Bahlul gets the form leader to do that while he plans the day's lessons.

Sally arrived. 'Has everyone heard? Camilla's not in.'

Bahlul fell to his knees, his hands raised.

We discussed the situation. Jim said he could probably manage Bahlul's Year 7s as well as supervising his own Year 13s next door.

Sally said no, she'd take the Year 7s.

'Stay on your knees, mate,' Jim said, and made Bahlul promise that he would bring us all presents from the States. 'No trinkets or tat.'

Bahlul repeated obediently, 'No trinkets or tat.'

Colin SpowerPoint for PHSE was all about exercises you can fit into a normal day, such as walking to the next bus stop or taking stairs instead of lifts. (I've accidentally deleted the body organs one. I swear, m'lud, my hand slipped.)

'See?' I said, targeting the bare hench crew. 'You don't need rowing machines or weights. Walk to the kitchen yourself instead of asking your mum to bring you a sandwich.'

They looked scandalized.

Stayed at school late, compiling grade reports and rough-planning lessons for the week after Easter, so that all I'll have to take home is marking. And Ofsted-angst.

And I have my reading diary article to finish.

Home at 7. Spouse out powerspeeding. When he came back, I was asleep on the sofa. He says he ate his spaghetti Bolognese while I snored.

At 9 p.m. woke up, microwaved my Bolognese, then gawped at the TV like someone crazed.

Compensation, though. No Friday school means no break duty! And Good Friday means hot cross buns!

As well as a time of contemplation and reflection on the sad events of the day, of course.

First half of summer term

Monday 16 April

Teacher training day. We'd had an email to say the Smuts had splashed out on Danish pastries for breakfast. Everyone came early to witness the phenomenon, like people turning up to watch the Aurora Borealis.

Jim, Sally and I found seats, carrying our coffees and pastries and discussing the day's agenda. Morning: a child psychologist on attachment disorders. Afternoon: reviewing departmental plan targets in our subject areas.

Reviewing departmental plan targets? I asked if someone could shoot me there and then – or perhaps once I'd finished my pastry.

'Did you two see the Bahlul presents in your pigeonholes?' Jim said.

We had. 'The boy done good,' Sally said, 'luckily for him.'

Nodded to Camilla as she arrived, pastry-free, and sat behind us. She's wearing a lot of foundation. The wrong colour for her. As though trying to look healthy.

Adrian gave his usual welcome-back speech devoid of cheer and hope, then introduced the psychologist. Her flaming red hair reminded me of one of Mum's wigs.

'Not more psychobabble,' I heard a science teacher mutter, but he went quiet when the psychologist displayed a photograph of a small child, crying, alone in a dark bedroom.

She told us that the interactions a small child has or doesn't have with primary caregivers set patterns for life. When young children cry and no one responds, or they're injured or abused and no one helps, or when a parent is unavailable because of substance abuse, children lose trust in the world.

They fear intimacy.

They hate to be needy.

They resist help.

My heart drummed in my chest. I couldn't look away from the photograph.

'But what happens to these children at school,' she asked us, 'when they display obnoxious behaviours? Disrupting. Acting out. Hurting others.'

Later, she distributed case studies and we formed groups of three. Sally, Bahlul and I discussed the cases. At least, they did.

Sally said, 'You're quiet. Is it the shock of being back?'

'Something like that,' I said.

Camilla was oddly officious during the afternoon, battering and slapping us with all the targets in the departmental plan we hadn't met, despite Jim's protests that many had been unrealistic.

Strange. I thought she'd softened.

Home at 7. Found Spouse pacing the kitchen, chanting Scripture while grilling fish.

'Hello, Jesus,' I said.

It didn't get the evening off to a good start, and I'm in bed now, writing this, and wondering why I can't be nice.

Tuesday 17 April

On the bus, read a chapter of *Fade* by Robert Cormier, about a teenager who discovers he can become invisible. Hoping to use it next year with a Key Stage 3 class. As long as they don't discover the secret, which would make classroom control interesting.

Sally says she thinks she ate twenty-two scones in Devon. 'I've put on three pounds,' she told me, Jim and Bahlul.

'They don't show,' I said. 'And you always lose anything you gain. I wish I could. Everything OK with Archie?'

'Not really,' she said. 'Hence the twenty-two scones.'

Jim broke into an awkward silence with a comment on the weather. We'd all seen the forecast. 'Snow on the ground at the beginning of the month,' he said, 'and now a heatwave coming.'

Bahlul thinks we're wimps when it comes to heatwaves. He says it's his one chance to feel superior.

My form is obsessed with the Year 11 prom in July. 'Your GCSEs are more important than your ball gowns and tuxes,' I said in registration. I may as well have said, *Kindly detach a limb and leave it at the door as you go out.*

Year 8 don't speak the same language as I do either. They heard 'This half-term we're analysing visual media for representational features' as 'We're watching movies for six weeks'.

No, I am not bringing popcorn.

Introduced Year 7 to Shakespeare's *The Tempest* by playing a soundtrack of thunder and lightning while they wrote about how it feels to be in a storm.

One seemed distracted. 'Miss, did you say the Taliban were in this play?' she said.

'No. Caliban. The island native. *Ca*liban.' Hopefully, Mum and Dad won't ring in now, asking why we're teaching about Islamic fundamentalists in English.

Most of Year 12 handed their Easter homework in. A relief. SIMS has been down since yesterday and we can't punish anyone until it's up again.

Gave the Coursework Five their new marks. Was able to award two or three more to all except Conor, who was right that he'd made his worse. We'll stay with his original mark.

'Did they take you long to re-mark?' one asked.

I may have exaggerated slightly.

Sent the marks to Camilla. Radio silence.

Proofread the reading diary article one more time and sent email to the editor.

Wrote a second email, attaching the article.

Wednesday 18 April

The mini-heatwave. Wore sandals today, but haven't painted my toenails yet after the winter. Kept my feet under the desk as much as possible.

Camilla found me in the library during Period 1, hiding behind a display of sci-fi books and marking Year 7 storm scenes. Had gone there to avoid Bahlul's chat, but it also helped with the toenail issue. Killed two birds.

Plus, the library is cooler. Three birds.

'Can we talk shapes?' Camilla said. She didn't sit down.

Ah. Ofsted.

'Have you tried horseshoes yet?' she said. She was quite loud and I wondered what the librarian was making of this conversation. 'Or clusters,' she added.

'Aren't clusters groups with a posh name, though?' I said.

She toyed with her jacket pocket and said she was putting sixth-formers into shapes from now on and it would be better if I could show solidarity.

'But they prefer the rows,' I said. 'They concentrate better. They can see the board. They don't distract each other . . . so much.'

'We decide what's best; not them. And – and Adrian prefers it.'

I said, 'They are young adults. I won't force them into shapes.'

Maybe 'won't' was a poor choice. She turned and left.

I did try with Year 13 later. 'How about a change of seating?' I said, trying to sound upbeat. 'In groups?'

'Oh, Miss, not you too,' Rebekah said, like Caesar said, '*Et tu, Bruté?*'

Son and DIL asked if I'd babysit, so I missed Bible study. Finished marking Year 7 and Year 12 work once the Littluns had stopped telling me they were too hot to go to sleep and that their bedroom doors were open just a millimetre too much/little/much/little/much.

Spouse has just said had I noticed how much better I slept over Easter and how much less I complained about spots?

Thursday 19 April

Told my form it would be the hottest day since 1949, according to the news.

'Was it really bad in 1949?' they said.

'I was not alive, you won't be surprised to learn.'

But some were.

Colin listened to me! This morning, Marion took an assembly on body image. She showed videos featuring interviews with a girl who'd been anorexic as a teenager and an eighteen-year-old boy who was trying to kick a steroid habit.

The audience had so many questions that we missed some of PHSE. Colin came to see why assembly was delayed (and why the Year 11s weren't in lessons yet, watching his muscles PowerPoint), but Marion shooed him away in a manner that thrilled us all.

A practice *Macbeth* exam for my Year 11 English class. They know it's serious now, with only a month until the real deal. I sat at the back, watching Danny, Jake and Ed stop start stop start stop start, moaning about stiffened fingers even after twenty minutes.

Free period sabotaged by Bahlul, who was in the office lecturing on American food, buses, sightseeing, hotels . . .

He was just getting started on American taxis, so I said, 'Shouldn't you be teaching now?'

His class was on a school trip.

Jim came in, saw Bahlul mid-flow, swivelled on his heels and disappeared.

Bahlul said, 'Why does no one want to hear my travel stories? Next time, you're all getting tacky ornaments.'

Year 8s very happy to analyse the opening section of a Garfield movie. 'This isn't proper work,' they said, while learning about camera angles, symbolism and diegetic sound.

Spouse has hurt his ankle so hasn't powersped for a couple of days. 'Hope I don't put that weight back on,' he said.

Told him I'd quite liked his paunch. Kind of cosy.

He said anyone would think I'd prefer an unfit, flabby husband who panted while climbing stairs.

'Don't be silly.'

Email from the *emagazine* editor. She likes the article. Publication September!

Friday 20 April

Thanked the Journos. They've been targeting my inbox all week with their Easter offerings. Said I'd check them aysap.

Lukas said, 'Did you just say aysap, Miss?'

'Maybe,' I said.

'Miss, you is well down with the yoof, isn't it?' he said. I felt proud, but then he said, 'Please don't do that again.'

They're all fascinated by Mr Vinnicombe's circus career.

'Did he have to wear a leotard?' Noora wanted to know. 'Eeurgh!'

'We didn't ask,' Samuel said, patiently.

Took Year 7 into a computer room I'd booked so we could research Shakespeare and benefit from air-con. Arrived to find a science teacher who'd chanced it and brought his Year 8s without reserving the room. He was taking his tie off and untucking his shirt.

My Year 7s cheered as he and his class left, tails between their legs.

Later in the lesson, one boy found out that Shakespeare had spelled his own name six different ways. I heard Lynne explaining that spelling hadn't yet been standardized. 'That's so unfair,' he said. 'Why wasn't I born then?'

He backtracked when another boy pointed out that he could have been forced to work in a factory, or been deported for stealing a loaf of bread, or died of the plaque.

'Plague,' I said, 'not plaque. But good point.'

Lynne said to me, 'Hope you're impressed with my knowledge of standardization. I've been watching some YouTube videos. Heard of David Crystal?'

'O blessed be his holy name,' I said, bowing.

'What?'

I said that if I ever divorced Spouse or he died, I would marry David Crystal.

'Doesn't he have a wife?' she said.

Told her not to complicate matters.

Year 12 complained to me about being forced into shapes by Miss Stent. She's clustered them in groups of three. Tried to show solidarity. 'She's encouraging you to be a rich resource to each other. To share your ideas and insights.'

Gus's expression said that he resents sharing oxygen, let alone ideas and insights.

A warm, sticky night. We had ice with the Baileys this evening and I marked books on the table in the garden. Am sure I won't sleep tonight.

Wish I knew more about my earliest years. What blood-family members I do have edge round the subject as people edge around chasms, and who can blame them? Chasms are places of echo, and who wants those kinds of echoes? But it means those years are a jigsaw, and I only have a few pieces. Dark pieces. Bits of night sky, perhaps. Or the thickest, deepest parts of a forest.

Monday 23 April

Was awake and in the shower at 5.30 a.m., then dozed on the sofa until Spouse woke me to say I'd be late.

Told Year 7 that, as tradition has it, Shakespeare died on this day. His birthday. They wanted to know how. I said that no one really knew for sure.

Perhaps, they suggested, his head dropped into his birthday trifle. Or he blew out candles, using so much breath he collapsed. Or he choked on a sausage roll. Or opened a birthday card, sustaining a paper cut that became infected, causing blood poisoning.

I said I thought the Shakespeare historians would be most grateful for their contributions towards the debate.

Year 8's homework had been to watch three film trailers on YouTube and rank them for effectiveness, with reasons. I'd given a possible list of ten films. Over half the class had watched and ranked all ten, dedicating much of their weekend to the process. 'Can we have homework like this all the time?' they said.

Lynne and I pronounced ourselves impressed with their diligence. But in the staffroom later, their maths teacher said, 'Year 8 tell me you gave them so much homework, they didn't have time to do mine.'

Treachery.

Macbeth revision with Year 11, reviewing their practice essays and learning quotations. 'Does anyone remember any of the witches' lines?' I said.

Danny volunteered. I was pleased, bearing in mind his rugby obsession means he rarely completes homework and does the minimum in lessons.

I smiled. 'Go on, Danny.'

He said, '"Foul is . . ." No, hang on. "Fair is foul and foul is fair. Hoover through the fog and filthy air."'

A chorus of '*Hoover?*' from his friends. 'You mean *hover!*'

Told Sally. She said, 'He will never be allowed to unsay that.'

The weather is unsettled again and cooler. The cardigans in my wardrobe don't know whether they're coming or going.

Tuesday 24 April

We all reckon Adrian slept through his alarm this morning. He had head-stubble, like when a field has been scorched. At least we had something to look at while he burbled on about Ofsted, saying nothing new.

Kate and William have had a third child, my form was keen to tell me. 'They'll call it Diana,' one girl said.

'It's a boy,' someone scornfully pointed out.

But the girl insisted that the old rules no longer applied. 'If they want to call a boy Diana, they should be able to.'

Uproar. For twenty-first-century teenagers, they're very *Daily Mail*.

Year 12 still determined to remain unshaped. Saw Camilla pass the classroom and peer in at the window. They chose that moment to look Victorian-schoolroom, bolt upright in their chairs as though I'd threatened them with ten strokes and a dunce cap.

In the department meeting, poor Sally was given only five minutes for her top tips about classroom psychology, how to create a positive learning atmosphere, and building morale. The remainder of the time Camilla devoted to further discussion of the departmental plan and how poorly we were implementing it.

Camilla's a real mixture these days, forgetting some things as though she no longer cares, and then being overly jobsworth and pedantic about others. We preferred her predictable.

When Camilla had gone, Jim said, 'Has she been banging on about shapes to anyone else?'

Jim and Sally share a Year 12 group. Sally shapes them, but always has. Jim says he teaches every class in rows, whether Year 7s or Year 13s. 'What's good enough for my allotment . . .' he said.

In my Year 13 lesson, Conor returned the penultimate version of his coursework that has a higher mark than the one he improved.

But Camilla has said nothing about the Year 13 coursework marks I sent her.

Spouse has bought some startlingly white new trainers for his powerspeeding. He's already worn out one pair.

'They are gangsta trainers,' I told him. 'You look like someone who deals drugs but only from the ankles down.'

Wednesday 25 April

Sally has judged the mini-saga competition and organized distribution of prizes.

She offered more help, but I told her she'd done enough. 'Just bring me cake as the deadline approaches. What would we do without you?'

'Thank my mother,' she said. 'She wouldn't let us have cake. Said it was indulgent. I've spent my life making up for lost time.'

'And spreading the joy among the rest of us,' I said. 'Don't ever leave me.'

Two emails arrived during my free in Period 5 while I was proof-reading Noora's article on bullying and trying not to let it un-nerve me. One was from the Art department and it had some twenty images attached, fully captioned with names and titles of pieces.

I sent over-effusive thanks.

The other was from James's form tutor to let me know James is in hospital with pneumonia after a chest infection over Easter. He won't be back for a fortnight.

Had two thoughts: 'Oh no, poor James!' and 'How will I get hold of all the magazine pieces saved on his school computer account?'

I may not have had the thoughts in that order.

Bible study this week was about the book of Lamentations. No danger of giggling. Lamentations isn't known for its gags.

Spouse said as he turned off his bedside lamp, 'If Sally offers you help, you're bonkers not to take it.'

'She's already given up loads of time', I said, 'that she can't afford.'

He's got his back to me now, but I'm sure he's not asleep.

Thursday 26 April

Didn't have to look in the mirror to know there was a clutch of spots rampaging on my jawline. Felt them, tender and stinging, as soon as the alarm shrilled me awake.

Mirror said, 'Whoa there!'

No eye contact made with Bathroom Scales. The day had begun badly enough.

Art and Photography GCSE exam days today, so PHSE lesson half empty. Was wondering whether to impose Colin SpowerPoint on them anyway when the Monster-girl tiptoed up to my desk and whispered, 'Can I tell the class about what happened? Do you think it would be helpful?'

I said, 'Only if you really want to. Don't feel any pressure.'

She shook her head. 'I've been preparing. In case.'

She stood at the front and began, 'How many of you are aware that most major UK supermarkets have recently banned the sale of energy drinks to under-sixteens?'

Only three were.

'Let me tell you why,' she said.

As she spoke about pressure to perform, and about self-harm, her voice was shaky and she pulled on her sleeve ends. The class listened silently. When she said, 'So that's my story,' they applauded her and whooped.

I gave her a merit, but it seemed small reward.

Email from Barbara while I was writing an introduction for the magazine. Could I pop into Adrian's office soon?

After email ping-pong, settled on Period 4 tomorrow.

Jim said, 'That sounds ominous.'

'Thanks,' I said. 'I'm about to breathe into a paper bag as it is.'

Zak looked happier today until I asked how Mum was and his face darkened.

Angel Child said, 'He won't want to talk about it, Miss.'

Felt ashamed to be so crass.

Sally said, 'Don't beat yourself up.'

Friday 27 April

My birthday. Fifty-five. Two score years and fifteen. Halfway to 110.

Twenty-one plus thirty-four?

Kept my head down to avoid Mirror. Suspected the chin spots were worse and didn't want confirmation.

'Denial won't help,' Mirror said.

'Today it will,' I said. 'Trust me.'

Spouse cooked me boiled eggs and soldiers for breakfast, even though it was only 6.30. I opened his presents: my favourite Coco Chanel perfume, a box of Milk Tray and a book voucher. 'You've made significant improvement', I said, 'since you bought me that ironing-board cover the first year we were married.'

Found Jim and Sally in the office and a chocolate cake balanced on my marking pile. Sally had piped 'Eat me' in pink icing.

She hugged me. I saw Jim hesitate, but then he hugged me too – a first. 'When in Rome,' he said. 'Happy birthday.' He peered at the message on the cake. 'It would be rude not to obey.'

'We'll be late for registration,' I said.

'Thirty seconds won't matter,' Sally said, and produced a cake knife.

She brought more cake with coffee to my break duty, which I was spending, disconsolate, standing beside two Year 7s who'd thought yelling in Anglo-Saxon at other Year 7s acceptable.

The Journos signed a Get Well card for James. Samuel seems bereft. Lukas is no substitute.

Went to see Adrian in Period 4. He's brought the deadline for the magazine forward by two days. 'I'm so sorry,' he said. 'But Barbara rightly reminded me we'd need a couple of days to distribute, as it's going to staff and governors as well as pupils.'

It is?

Emailed the printers after school to change timings and numbers, then planned next week's work. Rang Spouse to say I might be late for my birthday meal at Zizzis.

'Might?' he said.

'What time is it now?'

'Six forty-five.'

I asked what time we'd booked it for.

'Six thirty. I told you that. I'm already here, drinking red wine and looking very divorced.'

Monday 30 April

Camilla has reported me for non-shaping.

Let me tell myself that again.

Camilla has reported me for non-shaping.

Marion found me in the office at 9.30 a.m. eating leftover cake while proofreading magazine articles.

'My kind of breakfast,' she said, but I knew she wasn't there for small talk.

She sat in Sally's chair and told me Camilla was concerned about my unsupportive stance. Marion's voice lacked conviction. I suspect she doesn't like telling people off.

'I'm not trying to be difficult,' I said. 'It's the pupils. They honestly feel they learn better.'

'The problem is, it's a school-wide policy not to have sixth-formers in rows,' she said.

Later, Jim said, 'Don't take it too personally. Marion's tried to persuade me as well.'

Asked him whether Camilla had grassed him up too.

'She doesn't need to,' he said. 'Marion knows the way I work.'

There was a pause.

I said, 'What did you say to Marion?'

'I can't repeat it.'

'Oh, confidentiality?'

'No, obscenity.' He laughed.

Year 11 wrote an unseen poetry practice question. 'I'm never going to become an English teacher,' said one girl as I collected scripts in.

'Why not?'

'I'd hate to mark the trash I've just written,' she said.

Far too many of them nodded or groaned in agreement. But it's 11 p.m. now and I've put down my purple pen.

'They've been listening!' I said to Spouse, when he came upstairs.

He was pleased for me, but pointed out the time. 'You've marked for five hours solid. You're driving yourself too hard. It worries me.'

'Don't let it,' I said.

'It's like self-flagellation. Punishing yourself with marking rather than a cat-o'-nine-tails.'

How ridiculous.

Tuesday 1 May

Adrian was stubble-free but tense during briefing, stressed about Ofsted, exam results and league tables, and – bless him – happy to share the worry out.

The Head of Science said, 'Ofsted won't come during the exam period, surely? How would that work?'

'Of course they could. We'd have to make it work,' Adrian said, looking as though he didn't think it would work.

Fitted in some editing at break. James and Samuel were right. Paul Vinnicombe's interview is more about his circus career than his teaching, but probably better for it. And there's a photograph.

Jim suggested I caption it 'Beauchamp's Resident Swinger'.

Said I'd mull it over.

In Year 7's *The Tempest* lesson, they researched interpretations of the island native, Caliban, in the computer room. Unfortunately, some were more interested in his name being a near-anagram. Before we could stop them, they'd found distressing accounts of people eating each other.

The lunchtime meeting was awkward. Haven't spoken to Camilla since she betrayed me to the Smuts. She sat at my side, I think so she didn't have to meet my eyes. But I spent the meeting rotating on my swivel chair. That kept her busy.

Had told Year 13 to compile lists of quotations from literary critics about *Handmaid* and *The Road*. Conor brought one quotation. Made him look up 'list' in the dictionary and bunged him on SIMS for lack of work.

Most handed in homework essays. I'd given them a selection of titles to choose from. Rebekah had written three.

Son and DIL rang to invite us for dinner. 'I can't,' I whispered to Spouse, pointing at the piles of marking I'd unloaded on to the dining table.

'I'll come,' Spouse said into the phone. 'Leave Mum in peace.'

A quiet evening of marking. But no real peace.

Wednesday 2 May

I know I slept at some point last night because I dreamed that Matt and Conor helped me mark Rebekah's essays. Conor said, 'She's spelled it Handmaid's Tail!' and I snatched the paper and said, 'Let me see that.'

My tutees are meant to revise in registration period these days, but are still obsessed with prom arrangements. 'You do realize', I said, 'that the Year 11 prom is an American invention that we've borrowed.'

'Like Oreos?' someone said.

'Like Oreos.'

'And those Reese's peanut butter cups?'

'And those.'

'And elevators?'

'Yes,' I said. '*And* "I looked out the window" instead of "I looked out *of*". That one really annoys me.'

Class-wide bewilderment.

'You are all so young, it hurts,' I said.

Year 12 tell me that if they're studying AS subjects, with an exam this year, they've been told they can take the day off before that exam, so will miss some of my English lessons.

'It isn't proper study leave,' some complained.

I said, 'But you can't stop coming to your non-AS subjects entirely. How would I catch you up on so much material?'

'Year 13 have proper study leave.'

I explained that Year 13 were at the end of their courses.

'I don't have any AS exams this year,' one said. 'So I get no study leave.'

'Well, no,' I said. 'Because you're not revising yet. That'll be you next year.'

Seriously. It's like reasoning with a tray of baked potatoes.

I tried to sound positive. 'In June, you'll be starting on your coursework topic. You won't want to miss that. It'll be fun.'

'It won't,' one boy intoned. 'That's when the World Cup starts.'

After dinner tonight, I informed Spouse he'd have to go to Bible study alone for the next hundred years. 'I have so much marking and planning and magazine work, I don't know what to pick first.'

'Pick working part-time?' he suggested.

Thursday 3 May

Since Marion delivered the assembly to beat all assemblies a fortnight ago, Year 11's expectations have risen. Today's offering, 'Health for Revision' from Colin SpowerPoint, was ill-received. He takes monotone to new heights. Sally suggested a new career dubbing films about drones or bluebottles.

But not to him.

I switched off while he talked and thought back to what Bathroom Scales had said earlier: 'Three pounds on, I'm afraid. Still, that'll come off easily.'

'Not if she carries on like she is,' Mirror said. 'She rarely works up a sweat, to be frank.'

'Look at my chins,' I wailed, nodding up and down to see how they landed.

Mirror said. 'I'd keep looking straight ahead.'

Didn't have chance before the lesson to check the PHSE materials Colin sent. It turned out to be a worksheet containing three questions, which took Year 11 five minutes to complete. With fifty-five minutes to fill, found a YouTube documentary about people with exercise addiction. Watched it with the class. Decided that, even if my hips are broader than they could be, at least I don't wear my muscles and veins on the outside like something in the *British Medical Journal*.

Camilla away today and tomorrow. Jim says Marion says she's getting tetchy about Camilla's absences. She has too many exam classes getting a raw deal.

Friday 4 May

GCSE study leave starts next Friday. At Journos today, Aleesha said, 'It's my last day, Miss. I've sent you all my files.'

The rest asked if we'd still meet on Fridays after the magazine is out. 'Of course,' I said. 'We'll be the Senior Writing Club again.'

'Will Samuel still be able to come?' James asked.

'Miss will sort it somehow,' said Betsy.

James and Samuel high-fived.

Such faith. It's too heavy. How does God stand it?

Lukas said he'd be at a sports event next week. I hovered over him while he forwarded sports reports to me. His inbox was crammed with some he hadn't even looked at.

In other news, James has agreed from his hospital bed that IT staff can retrieve his *Beauchamp Matters* folder from the school network.

My inbox and my own *Beauchamp Matters* folder are filled with pieces half finished, quarter finished and barely started, half accurate, quarter accurate and barely accurate. It's like clearing up confetti after a wedding, scattered all over paths and gravestones, in bushes, inside the church porch and up a tree.

Bahlul's interview needs editing. He told Noora and Betsy his motivations for teaching were holidays and going home by 4. 'It's the truth!' he told me after school while dropping exercise books haphazardly into a bag. 'Plus, I like being in the classroom with the kids.'

I said he probably should have mentioned that.

'Add it in if you like,' he said.

When he'd gone, Sally asked me what I was doing for the weekend. Told her we were staying in Isleworth, seeing the family. 'I'm taking all the magazine editing,' I said.

'Email me some proofreading,' she said. 'Seriously. It'll be a laugh, if nothing else. And Archie's away again.'

'Where's he going?'

'Some work conference, he says.' She turned to close her laptop.

'On a bank holiday weekend?'

She didn't respond to that.

'It's not fair to give you proofreading,' I said. 'You weren't the fool who volunteered for the magazine.'

'No,' she said, 'but I'm friends with the fool who did. Aren't I?'

Tuesday 8 May

Hottest early May bank holiday since records began.

Arrived home late last night, having learned that only contortionists can edit magazines on laptops while on sweltering replacement buses from Bicester North to Banbury.

Another annoyance: my two daughters talked about me to Spouse in the third person while I was there. It was like being in my bathroom.

'Dad, why did you let her volunteer for this magazine palaver?' YoungerDaughter said as we sat watching TV.

'I didn't,' he said. 'I told her not to.'

OlderDaughter said, 'Surely she has enough to do with all the other schoolwork. I can't believe she's actually brought marking. There's a pile of books on my kitchen table.'

I said, 'Only a little pile.'

'Of course she has enough to do,' Spouse said. 'She worked seventy-three hours last week. I calculated she earned less than a paper boy.'

'Hello.' I waved at my family. 'Hello. Is it me you're looking for?'

Spouse has just said to me before he turned his lamp off, 'They're worried, that's all. Like I am.'

Teachers and pupils alike confused today, thinking it Monday. Adrian not happy, as several teachers were missing from briefing. He told us that Ofsted are visiting two local schools this week. He said it in the way police would report an escaped tiger in the Luton area.

'Did you notice his tie?' Jim asked me and Bahlul before our lunchtime meeting.

'Hard not to,' I said. 'I think we were all gazing at his chest.'

'Don't sport a balloon-patterned novelty tie, then, when you usually wear beige,' Bahlul said.

'He's realized he's boring,' Sally said, coming in.

But Camilla was right behind her, lips pursed, and shut us up by allotting tasks. Apparently, I'm organizing the Year 7 exam next week: preparing comprehension passages, questions and mark schemes. Compiling. Collating. Photocopying. Distributing. Moderating.

Because I have so much spare time.

Jim says that Camilla has been 'spoken to' by the Smuts about absences.

'How do you know?' we asked him.

But we knew how he knew.

Wednesday 9 May

Mirror told me my complexion looked grey this morning.

'It's lack of sleep,' I said.

'Or lack of common sense in knowing when to say no.'

Asked Mirror to stick to its normal job, but there's no avoiding the fact that the grey complexion makes this week's three spots (forehead, cheek, chin) more noticeable.

'Do you think my face looks like putty?' I asked Spouse when he came downstairs to make coffee. 'Putty with acne?'

He said he couldn't comment. He'd never seen putty with acne, as it usually came with window frames.

Spent both free periods on the magazine. Called IT several times for help with image cropping, page margins and spacing. I think they dread my calls.

Then received an email from Adrian. Subject heading: Magazine. My heart went bee-doop in case he said he'd just found a list he wrote. But it was a foreword for the magazine (unsolicited). 'Barbara has proofread it,' his email said, 'so you can print as is.'

Not saying it was dreary, but I've seen more exciting prose in the small print of my phone contract.

Last lesson with Year 13s before study leave. Rebekah brought in vegan cake made with parsnips and I think millet or fragments of balsa wood. Fortunately, one of the other girls brought in proper cake. Matt and Conor had signed a card saying, 'Sorry, Miss, for everything!' which was quite sweet, but might also mean they're not intending to come to revision sessions.

Thursday 10 May

No sign of Ofsted yet. Perhaps another school has locked the inspectors in a science cupboard. Hope springs.

They miss me at Bible study, Spouse told me this morning while lacing his trainers for a morning trek. 'And me,' he said. 'I miss you too.'

'And me,' I said. '*I* miss me.'

His trainers aren't as pristine now. And we've washed all his white sports socks with my new purple shirt. Not such a convincing gangsta look.

Year 11 PHSE lessons are now revision periods. A relief, in some ways. I've found PHSE draining, although persuading thirty teenagers to revise peacefully isn't a walk in the park either. Had to threaten detentions.

Last official Year 11 English lesson. We played 'literary terms' hangman and 'Guess the quotation', and they teased Danny about the hoovering witches again. I passed round tubs of mini-flapjacks and Haribo.

'It's not a final goodbye, remember,' I said. 'Revision sessions continue in normal lesson times. You're expected to attend each one if you don't have other exams.'

I saw Ed and Jake exchange glances. Like *that's* happening.

Mentioned PHSE to Jim at break time while we drank coffee and I pecked at my keyboard, adding in some apostrophes and deleting others. 'Draining?' he said. 'Why?'

Tried to backtrack. 'Oh, I don't know. It rakes things up, that's all.'

'Go on.'

Could I say?

I was glad I wasn't facing him. 'I'll tell you some other time. Better crack on.'

'OK. No worries,' he said. He sounded hurt, though. As if I'd slapped him.

Year 8 not pleased to find that today's lesson and tomorrow's are exam preparation and not the opening credits of *Shrek 2*. They took a while to calm down.

Leon is playing up again. He's much better behaved when he's a monster. But his article for *Beauchamp Matters* is charming. I thanked Lynne, who'd helped him.

Clean out of Baileys. 'That bottle went down quick,' Spouse said, watching me empty the last drops into a glass, but fortunately he was halfway through a meditation on a psalm.

'I won't disturb you,' I said, and tiptoed upstairs to the study.

Friday 11 May

In school just after dawn broke to prepare Year 7 exams. Surprised to find Camilla there. She looked tired, her face strained.

'Ah,' she said, awkwardly. (She's mentioned nothing further about shapes, but the issue drifts between us like a spook.) 'I was hoping you'd arrive.'

Oh?

She said, 'I'm afraid I need you ... need your help.' She told me Year 13 have been asking her for revision lessons on their Shakespeare play, studied with Pam last year. Camilla has put them off. She's never taught *Hamlet* before, but didn't want to admit it. 'I thought I'd have time to catch up. But I've been ...'

Here goes, I thought. *She's going to explain about her absences.*

But she didn't.

'There's not much time,' I said. 'That exam's on the seventh of June.' How come she'd left this so late? 'Presumably they've revised *Paradise Lost*.'

'A little.' A quick red blush took hold of her upper chest and neck. 'You know both texts back to front, don't you?'

I offered to go through them both with her so she could take the revision sessions.

'I'd rather you took them,' she said. 'Please. We'll tell them I have medical appointments. I can't bear fumbling through. They'll notice.'

(Especially you, Rebekah.)

So next week, in my two frees on Wednesday, I'm revising *Hamlet* with Year 13. And perhaps *Paradise Lost* the following week.

Camilla's taking some of my Key Stage 3 lessons in return, which, as bargains go, isn't exactly late Friday in Lidl.

I don't like the idea of lying about medical appointments. I'll stay vague.

She also asked me not to tell the rest of the department. I said I wouldn't, but how will they not notice? They'll see the books on my desk. Not even English teachers read *Paradise Lost* for fun.

Do they?

Final Journos session, tying up loose ends so I can get the copy ready to send off. Samuel spotted an 'it's' that should have been an 'its' and spent a happy five minutes explaining why to the others.

Study leave started today for Year 11s and 13s. They had emotional leavers' assemblies, giving Kleenex half their year's sales. Someone set off a fire alarm later, which meant trooping outside with Year 9 and then trying to refocus them on the lesson when they were as high as skyscrapers.

Year 13s were in fancy dress. Rebekah wore a Handmaid costume and looked as sinister as anything.

Sally hasn't brought cake in for a while.

Monday 14 May

Spouse ate Sunday lunch at Son's again yesterday while I put finishing touches to magazine copy. 'The Littluns asked where you were,' he said when he came back. 'They've made you this card.' It bore a picture of a unicorn, and Grandboy had written in large round letters, 'We kepe missing you Grandmar.'

Slid it under my laptop in case I thought about it too hard.

Woke in shock at 3 this morning. Dreamed I'd missed the printing deadline.

In real life, got to school early. Walking through the gates, I could see caretakers wheeling trolley-loads of chairs to the school's gym on the edge of the site, ready for the first GCSE exams today.

In the office, checked the instructions from the printers again. They said: 'We prefer PDF files to Word.'

Read it again. 'We prefer PDF files to Word.'

It was still there the third time. My stomach dropped. How did I miss that?

Don't panic, I told myself. *Trust in the Lord. Have faith. Put your hope in Him. He will provide.*

But, just in case, I ate two Penguin biscuits I had in my stationery drawer.

Kev from IT found me palpitating by his door with my laptop when he arrived at 8.30. 'I'll bring you presents tomorrow,' I said. 'Wine. Chocolates. Exotic pets. Just take pity.'

He ordered a box of Celebrations, then I sat beside him.

It took fifteen minutes.

'What?' I said. 'I thought that would take all morning. All day.'

'Not these days. Keep up,' he said.

I let all the breath I owned out of my lungs. 'Kev, you are practically Jes– A miracle-worker.'

'No dumbing down the chocolates, mind,' he said.

I pressed Send at 9.30 a.m. Sally was in the office, marking. 'It's gone,' I said.

She turned. 'What has?'

'The magazine.'

'No! Gone where?' she said.

'I mean, good gone. Gone to the printers.'

She put her hand to her sternum. 'Don't do that to me.'

I checked the clock. 'I'd better go. I'm invigilating a Year 8 exam.' I yawned as I stood up. It was a ten-seconder.

'Welcome back,' Sally said when I'd finished.

My week's itinerary: Invigilate internal school exams either in the hall or in classrooms. Run GCSE and Year 13 exam revision sessions. Teach Year 12. Mark school exams. Moderate school exams. Dream about exams.

But – no more magazine!

Feel as though I've lost weight.

Tuesday 15 May

I *have* lost weight. Only a pound but, as Bathroom Scales said, big trees, little acorns.

Stopped off at shop for Kev's chocolates and bought myself a Fruit & Nut bar to celebrate the weight loss.

Staff briefing was a repeat of last week's. Adrian could have recorded himself then and sent it round as an MP3 file, Bahlul suggested.

To us, afterwards.

Adrian wore a Simpsons tie today. So why can't he talk and write like a Simpsons tie person?

Email from printers arrived while I was in the office distributing Year 7 exam scripts to colleagues.

It read, 'Does the magazine have a cover?'

Had to run to invigilate an exam. Spent the time prowling the aisles with sweaty palms, praying I hadn't lost the file. Then on to Year 11 revision session: half a class because of exams and perhaps because of apathy and Fortnite.

At lunch, after the department meeting, I dug the cover file out from the bowels of my laptop. Ran to see Kev in Period 5, taking his Celebrations with me. His colleague asked me to wait. Kev was currently rescuing a science teacher, trained in the days of quill and blackboard, from an interactive whiteboard disaster.

'Yes! My chocolates are here,' Kev said on his return.

'One more favour first,' I said, holding the box behind my back.

Wednesday 16 May

Year 13 had made a unilateral decision to unshape themselves, aware that I was running their revision session instead of Miss Stent.

Matt and Conor were missing.

'Let's crack on,' I said, hoping to forestall awkward questions about hospital appointments. '*Hamlet*, then. First, we'll revise critical opinions. Then consider major themes. Does anyone need paper? A pen?'

'Why are you talking so fast?' one boy said.

Camilla invigilated a Year 9 exam on my behalf during Period 2 so I could mark some Year 7 scripts. Honestly thought she'd pull a sickie in case Year 13 spotted her around school, but maybe Jim is right about what he says Marion says, and Camilla's been warned about absence.

Saw Year 13 again in Periods 3 and 4, my normal slots with them. Still no Matt or Conor.

Rebekah hung back at the beginning of lunch. Could she ask a question?

'Of course.' I expected a literature query.

'Which church did you say you go to, Miss?'

I busied myself tidying papers so she couldn't see the terror in my eyes.

She said, 'I mean, for a start, are there any young people?'

I said, 'Hm . . . young?' as though I needed a dictionary definition.

She was patient. 'Under thirty, say?'

I told her there were a few, but tried to make it sound like a real disappointment.

She pulled out her phone. 'Can you tell me the church's name?'

I surrendered it, in the manner of someone giving away £100 notes or a kidney, and she tapped it in.

'Ah, here's the website. Thanks, Miss. See you after lunch for *Hamlet*.'

Spent Period 5 talking about *Hamlet* with my mouth, but my mind was busy hoping (a) no one would ask why Miss Stent had just hurtled past the window and (b) Rebekah would have checked the church website pictures and focused on the grey-haired people.

Sloped along to Bible study, feeling like a stranger. Have missed so many. But three chocolate biscuits in and it was like old times.

Thursday 17 May

There's a spot on the end of my nose like the cherry on a Bakewell tart. Can see it out of my peripheral vision. Don't even have to cross my eyes.

'I thought you liked cakes,' Mirror said.

'Not fixed to my face, thank you.'

Haven't got back on Bathroom Scales. Just in case.

Exam papers are stacking up on our desks, like surreptitious layers of snow that become an avalanche and a rescue team and three St Bernards before you know it. We can't mark them fast enough, despite extra free periods during school exam week. Our only comfort is Sally's lemon drizzle cake. She made up for not bringing cake for a while by putting neat gin in the drizzle. It cheered us all. (Except you, Camilla, because you are anti-cake. And because you don't seem able to be cheered right now.)

Jim asked Sally if she could make a whisky-flavoured drizzle next time.

She said, 'Hm. Plenty of that in our drinks cupboard. Archie has expensive tastes.'

Camilla asked me, when no one else was in the office, how the revision sessions had gone yesterday.

I gave her three copies of the resource packs I'd prepared. 'You might want to send those to Matt and Conor. And there's one for you.'

'Pardon?' She looked at the papers as though she hadn't heard.

'Matt and Conor. They'll need these,' I said. It was as if I'd woken her up. Her eyes were not focusing. 'Are you all right, Camilla?'

She mumbled, 'Fine,' and left the office, clutching the papers.

Was she slurring her words? 'Revision sessions' did not come out right. Adrian would never have managed it without spitting on the assembly front row.

Ten Year 11s in Period 2. The others were either in exams, in preparation for exams or in McDonald's. We played a fun game of 'Guess who is where', then revised *A Christmas Carol*. Their first exam is next Tuesday. They are twitchy, like birds when bigger birds are near.

Throughout the writing of this diary entry, I've had a mega-blob of toothpaste in my peripheral vision.

Friday 18 May

Had an email from the printers, attaching the proofs. 'Do you want me to double-check them for you?' Sally asked.

I said she had enough to do.

'No worries,' she said. 'You know where I am if you need me.'

Two forty-five-minute periods of invigilation, the first in the Year 7 Geography exam. The pupils looked white-faced. The week of exams has sucked the light and glow from their lives. The lead invigilator sat at a desk on the stage, glaring at anyone whose pencil rolled inexorably from a desk to the floor.

Traversed the aisles feeling like Dickens' Gradgrind and trying not to fold my hands behind my back. But what else? Swing them? Fold them in front like a footballer nervously defending a penalty?

Invigilation is the pits. You know you're bored when a request for paper gives you a palpitation and a boost to self-esteem.

Later, half of my Year 12s were missing because of AS exams, although all the Privates were there. Gus was very quiet. His cheek looked bruised.

Jim told me in the office that a Year 12 boy has been excluded for punching Gus in the school dining room. It's Beauchamp's 'Healthy Eating Week' and apparently Gus mocked another sixth-form boy for not knowing what quinoa was, or how to say it.

Jim pronounced it 'queen noah'. 'Have I got that right?' he said.

'I think it's kee-noir, but I'm not really sure. Is anyone?' I said.

He said that Gus clearly thought he was.

No lunchtime clubs today because of exam week. It seemed odd, not being in the computer room peering over someone's shoulder at their screen.

Two free periods for marking, except that Bahlul was also in the office, marking but not marking. Tried my best to fend off his chatter, but in the end took refuge in the darkened corner of a physics lab.

Have spent the evening checking the proofs. Sent them back. Squinting at the diary now, my eyes sore.

My nose is sore too. The cherry spot is lingering. Applied dollop of toothpaste, but accidentally transferred it on to Spouse's forehead when he climbed into bed. He's gone to wash it off.

Monday 21 May

On Saturday morning, Spouse persuaded me away from exercise books to Warwick market. Met Son, DIL and Littluns for a pub lunch, TV screens broadcasting Harry and Meghan's wedding.

'I feel abnormal being normal at a weekend,' I said to Spouse while helping Grandgirl butter her roll.

Year 11's first Literature exam tomorrow. Alarmingly, in class today, two thought the first exams were English Language and have done no home revision of *A Christmas Carol* or *Macbeth*.

'But it's on your exam timetable,' I said. 'And I've reminded you most lessons.'

'I'm not sure where my copies of the texts are,' one boy said. 'They might be at my dad's.'

Asked him where his dad lived.

'Aberdeen.'

'The texts are both online,' I said, trying to stay patient. Offer solutions.

'We've just moved house,' he said. 'Mum hasn't got internet yet.'

The boy next to him wasn't as patient. 'Well, you're gonna bomb, then, aren't you?'

What had I thought of Meghan's dress? the girls wanted to know, although one said her dad refuses to watch anything about the Royals.

'Why?' the others asked.

'Because he's not a royalist,' she said. 'He's a publican.'

Year 8 delighted to be back analysing film techniques. We watched the opening credits of *Shrek 2* and identified camera angles. Goater noticed that her neighbour had written 'low angel shot' and shrieked it to the class. Kept her behind afterwards and asked her not to embarrass other pupils like that.

'But what if they're idiots?' she said, and I knew she meant it.

Spoke to her form tutor later in the staffroom.

'Didn't you meet her parents back in March?' she said.

'No. They missed their appointment and refused to wait for a free slot.'

'I met them a while back,' she said. 'The girl came too. I've never heard a mother criticize a child like she does. Sniping at her every move. Demanding perfection. The you-came-second-why-not-first type. The father uncomfortable with the whole thing.'

Tuesday 22 May

Adrian didn't mention Ofsted this morning. The menu was different.

Starter:

Department budgets are being cut again with immediate effect.

Main:

Reasons why.

More reasons why.

Further reasons why.
Dessert:
Implications of budget cuts.
More implications.
Further implic–

Stopped taking it in, like when you eat a Christmas dinner four times the size of a normal dinner, and suddenly can't eat another sprout, or sultana. Down goes the cutlery, even though your mother-in-law looks daggers at you.

Adrian beckoned me over at the end to tell me that, although he appreciated all my efforts, budget cuts meant *Beauchamp Matters* would probably remain a one-off project. The governors had already hinted so. Wasn't sure how to arrange my face. Disappointed? Devastated? Resigned? Relieved?

'What was all that about?' Sally said in the office, so I told her.

'So much for Beauchamp *Matter*ing,' she said. 'The governors will regret that decision when they see the magazine.'

I said she shouldn't count her chickens.

She mock-slapped me. 'You are so annoying.'

Met Danny and other Year 11 boys in the corridor after today's Literature exam. Asked them how they'd coped with the question about Macbeth and his friend Banquo.

'They were *friends*?' Danny said. 'But doesn't Macbeth have him killed? When were they friends?' He looked perplexed.

'C'mon, mate,' one of his companions said, pulling on Danny's sleeve. 'Let's get some food and you can forget all about *Macbeth* until you do the resit next year.'

Wednesday 23 May

Paradise Lost revision with Year 13. Conor was there (we pretended not to recognize him), but told us Matt was 'inverted commas ill'.

Rebekah said, 'People in glass houses,' but that was lost on Conor.

Year 13 agreed that Satan comes out pretty well in Milton's epic religious poem and wondered how the God/Milton conversation went when he reached heaven.

'Awks,' one said. 'I bet Milton was bricking it.'

We moved quickly on.

Passed Reception at break time to see boxes stacked against the wall. A receptionist smiled. 'I'm told this is your fault,' she said. 'Do you want a copy before we start distributing?'

She fetched scissors and slit open a box.

Took *Beauchamp Matters* to the office. The smell of printing ink made my eyes water.

'Let me see it, let me see it,' Sally said, and sat beside me as we flicked through. She kept oohing and aahing.

'Let's see the inside front page again,' she said. 'Hey, look at that. Your name in lights. Editor.'

I looked at her. 'But –'

She said, 'What? What is it? You've gone a sicky colour.'

I said, 'How did I forget to include acknowledgements?'

'Did you?'

'I haven't credited anyone else,' I said. 'The Journos. You. And the Head of Games. Staff, for volunteering for profiles. No one.'

'Never mind that,' she said. 'I don't need crediting. But – I guess – your Journos . . .'

I'd even written it down on a list somewhere. I knew I had. So, how –

'Don't worry,' she said. She started turning the pages again. 'Let's check again. You *must* have . . .' She looked at the inside back cover.

Told her not to bother. 'It's not there.' I glanced down at the page she had open. The head's foreword.

No! I pointed. 'And there's this,' I said, jabbing at it with my finger. Felt my eyes stinging.

'What?' she said.

At the bottom of the foreword, the name: Adrain Parkes.

She said, 'A *drain*? Oops.'

When Jim came in seconds later, I was sobbing like a child.

Couldn't concentrate on lessons for the rest of the day. Rookie behaviour control.

Didn't go to Bible study. Stayed at home to email apologies to all the unacknowledged. Spouse said before he left, 'Don't beat yourself up. It's an easy mistake.'

I said that there were two mistakes and hadn't he been listening? But he still poured me a glass of wine before he left, and kissed the top of my head.

Thursday 24 May

'Have I been asleep?' I asked Mirror this morning.

It said I looked as though I'd been in bed and messed myself up but stayed awake while doing so.

Reply emails dribbled in all day, most of the Journos saying they didn't even know what acknowledgements were. The Heads of Games and Art both spectacularly unbothered. Sally replied, 'Why have you even emailed me? I've already told you I don't need thanking.' Marion said, 'Ha ha!' and that the Head's brain was too full of Ofsted to be worried about tiny errors, so not to lose sleep.

Staff stopped me in corridors to say they'd got their copy and well done. No one made drain jokes.

James emailed to say he's officially back in school after half-term but would be popping in to see us Friday lunchtime. Think he secretly wanted to be acknowledged. 'You could publish an addendum,' he wrote.

'That's just wrong,' said Jim at break. He'd brought a piece of flap-jack to my classroom where I was marking. 'No Year 10 should know what an addendum is. Anyway, the magazine's already distributed.'

He's been very caring since he found me doing backstroke in my own tears yesterday.

Email from Adrain arrived during lunch, but all it said was, 'Delighted with the magazine. Pop into my office at some point.' He sounded happy, but was it a smokescreen?

Camilla took my Year 8s. They played her up, the traitors, even with Lynne there, and very little work was done. I've now got three of them for detention during break duty tomorrow.

Friday 25 May

Camilla offered to take my Year 7s for their *Tempest* lesson. I politely declined. The last thing I wanted was detained Year 7s trailing behind me at break as well as three Year 8s. What suited the Pied Piper doesn't suit everyone.

'But I thought you'd want to do half-term grade reports,' Camilla said.

Aarrgh. I forget them *every time.* Told her I'd stay after school if need be.

'Don't you have your club Friday lunchtimes?' she said. 'You've a busy day.'

'Honestly, it's fine,' I said.

She didn't remind me that the report deadline was 4 p.m. She is letting things slide, like someone no longer able to grip.

Zak's foster parents are taking him to Spain at half-term. He's worried about leaving his mum, though. He says she's at home, but doesn't get dressed.

Detained the Year 8s at break and made them do apostrophe worksheets as well as fill in my forms.

Ex-Journos Club at lunchtime. I had creative writing tasks ready, but they'd all brought their magazine copies and pored over them, pretending they weren't reading and re-reading their own pieces.

Samuel now has permission to go to Second Lunch so that he can stay with us. Lukas slapped him on the back and Samuel nearly fell over.

Everyone was pleased to see James. He's looking leaner and even more child prodigy. Samuel's face was pink with pleasure.

Two Year 11 girls poked their heads in to tell me about their Literature exam. 'They gave us Eric, Miss,' one said, 'for the *Inspector* question.'

The other said, 'I used the quote "half-sly, half-assertive" about Eric, Miss. Are you proud?'

'I am. Very,' I said.

They went off, hand in hand.

Half-*shy*. Not half-sly.

SIMS crashed during Period 4, deleting my Year 7 grades. Gave up on SIMS and went to see Adrain.

'The governors want me to pass on their thanks', he said, 'for your sterling work. And for mentoring the three Pupil Premium children. Here's a small gift to acknowledge your efforts.'

Acknowledgement? Risky ground!

He passed me a bottle bag. 'I hope you like Baileys.'

Cue dispassionate face. 'A treat is always welcome,' I said.

'By the way,' he said, holding the door open for me. 'Your instincts for the magazine were right. More pupils. Less PR.'

'Oh, I –'

'The human touch,' he said. 'It's not my forte.'

Tried to look truly astonished.

Email arrived at 4 p.m. SIMS refusing to be cured, even by Kev & Co. Grade reports postponed until after half-term.

Yay! Like finding a toffee in your pocket.

Second half of summer term

Monday 4 June

Clear skin after a week off school and reading two more Robert Cormier books. Spouse said it was fascinating that such tragic, unhappy books cheered me up.

Bathroom Scales reported two pounds on this morning, which cheered me down again.

Mirror said, 'Looks like insomnia is worse for your skin but better for your waistline.'

If only Mirror didn't sound so happy about these observations.

Introduced Year 8 to travel writing. 'What's been your most exciting holiday?' I asked.

'I've swum with dolphins,' one said.

'Really?' I said. 'I mean, how many of us have had the chance to do that?'

Seven put their hands up. As did Lynne. Others have scuba-dived, climbed mountains, swum in waterfalls and surfed.

'I did a holiday for deprived kids that the social worker sent me on,' said one of the front row boys, 'and sailed down a cliff.'

'Do you mean abseiled?' I said.

'Yeah. Abseiled. It was brilliant, except the straps cut into my meat and two veg.'

Five minutes later, we got the lesson back on track.

Double period of English Language revision with Year 11 ready for Paper 1 tomorrow. Half a class again, but three said they now understood how to approach the exam in a way they hadn't before.

I said I didn't know why. I hadn't explained it any differently.

One said, 'No, but I listened differently. Or, maybe I just listened.'

All very reassuring, I'm sure. I've only been teaching them for two years.

Stayed after school to input the postponed half-term grades and mark Year 13 practice essays. Everyone else had gone home – even Sally.

Ate all the Milky Ways from a box of Celebrations Jim had brought in. It was his birthday today. They're the box's diet option.

Three emails from teachers saying they'd enjoyed reading *Beauchamp Matters* over the holiday. 'Refreshingly free of puff pieces,' one said. And the Religious Studies department is basing a unit of lessons around some of the opinion articles.

At home, pressed Send on a short story, a submission for an anthology to be published later this year. Nothing ventured.

Spouse has just asked me what it was about. I said it was about a woman who kills her husband, but I told Spouse not to worry. I couldn't murder him until he'd taught me where the shed key was and how to empty the vacuum cleaner.

Tuesday 5 June

First throbbing spot of the half-term festering on the edge of my top lip. 'It hurts to smile,' I said to Mirror, while practising a half-smile.

'Just smile with your eyes,' Mirror said.

Adrain's briefing was Ofstedly tedious again. On the other hand, he did congratulate me on the magazine and led everyone in applause. Embarrassing, especially as I could only smile with my eyes.

He said, 'I'm hoping we can feature the magazine and its creators in a forthcoming assembly.'

He *is*?

Pats on the back from several colleagues. Sally rebuked me in the corridor. 'Stop saying it was all down to the Journos, please. It's not true.'

Two Year 11 girls came to the English office, bewildered by a question in this morning's English Language exam. 'We've failed,' one said. 'They asked us about this character called Rosabel in a story and whether she was right to be angry. We didn't know. Nobody knew.'

'I'm sure you did absolutely fine and are worrying unnecessarily,' I said, and gave them a chocolate each.

Looked on Twitter later. Half the country's teenagers bewildered by Rosabel.

Planned *The-Road*-and-*Handmaid* comparison revision for Year 13, but they asked for more *Paradise Lost* instead.

'I've just ad-libbed Milton for a whole hour,' I said to Sally and Jim after school. 'I didn't know I could do that.'

'That's what you need,' Jim said, a hand on my shoulder. 'A bit more self-belief.'

'Seconded,' Sally said.

Felt emotional and oddly ashamed.

Spouse listened to medieval monk music all evening while I collated my Years 7, 8 and 12 school exam marks upstairs. I may have had the better deal for once.

Wednesday 6 June

Arrived early this morning and found Sally already in the office, putting on mascara. But her eyelids were puffy.

She told me why. She's discovered that Archie is a gambler. She found a casino receipt. 'That bank holiday work trip', she said, 'was a three-day gamble-fest in France with friends.'

I hugged her, then fetched us both a coffee.

'How can I have missed it?' she said, gulping it down. 'I've been living with him for a year. How come I didn't know?'

'But you didn't know to look,' I said.

'I really want to believe in him,' she said. 'To trust him.'

Gus Private is humbler these days. We've started on their language investigation coursework. He wants to write about rhetoric in political speeches.

'What's rhetoric?' asked one of the girls.

I could sense Gus suppressing a mansplain. He glanced my way.

'Check your glossary,' I said to her. 'It'll be there.'

Said to Bahlul at break, 'I'd never recommend getting thumped as character-building, but it's worked for Gus.'

Should have guessed Bahlul would have a related story.

Last ever lesson with Year 13. They have one exam tomorrow afternoon and the other next Tuesday. Rebekah brought a heavy cold, plus tolerable homemade vegan ginger shortbread and two more practice essays. She said, 'Cad I fetch them toborrow borning before the exab? I deed to check I'b doig the right thig.'

One of the others said that she'd been 'doig the right thig' since she slid from the woob.

'I'll mark them next period,' I said to her. 'Come to the office after school.'

Had anyone else brought practice essays?

No. Just you, Rebekah.

She knocked on the office door later as I wrote my last comment on her work. She'd brought a thank you card. It said, 'Might even see you at church!'

Spouse Bible studied tonight while I prepared resources for Year 11 revision. Spent time later, with a glass of Rioja, idly Googling 'attachment issues'. Came across more research suggesting that children whose parents mistreat them may go on to intimidate and bully others. That's how they feel significant. Seriously neglected children also push help away, it said. They're afraid – ashamed – to be needy in case the needs aren't met. They learn this lesson early.

Thursday 7 June

Couldn't remember having been asleep last night. And my throat was like sandpaper. (Here's looking at you, Rebekah.)

Said good morning to Spouse when he came down to make tea and he didn't hear me.

'How are you going to teach like that?' he said.

'Badly?' I mouthed.

'Stay at home,' he said, 'like normal people would.'

Had to cover a Year 7 science lesson before break. Wrote on the board, 'I cannot speak, but can run detentions and drag people to headteachers. Please work quietly.' It was risky. Year 7s now aren't what they were in September. But the threats plus a pig of a worksheet on diffusion focused their minds.

After lunch, gave Year 8 and Year 7 their English exam papers back and helped them record marks and future targets. Had hoped Lynne would stand in for my voice, but she was off sick. Struggled through with a combination of mime, instructions written on the board and impersonating Gollum.

Year 7 Zak scored only 23 per cent. He cried. Angel Child passed him a tissue. I forgot to ask about his week in Spain.

Twilight teacher training after school. Attachment Part 2. The red-haired psychologist played us a film she warned might be distressing. It showed researchers separating toddlers from parents, and tracking the children's reactions. Felt ill anyway by then, so the hammering of my heart could have been that.

Checked Year 12 coursework proposals tonight while drinking Lemsip and brandy. Very pleased with them, although Spouse said my judgement may have been warped.

Encouraged that they've all listed David Crystal, O blessed be his holy name, as a linguist they'll quote to support their ideas.

I wonder if Crystal already has an agent.

Friday 8 June

Woke at 5, sneezing and coughing, and feeling hot cold hot cold hot cold.

Spouse woke up.

'I can't go to school,' I whispered.

'Hurrah! Sense!' he said.

Spent an hour downstairs devising cover work for four lessons and emailing it to Camilla. Copied it to Sally. At 7.30, left hoarse message on the cover supervisor's answerphone. Spouse went gardening. I slipped back into bed.

7.45: Text from Sally: 'You poor thing. We all miss you. BTW, Camilla not here either.'

8.30: Couldn't get comfortable, so moved to sofa with duvet.

9.30: Remembered break duty and phoned the cover supervisor to arrange replacement.

10.45: Remembered my lunchtime club and texted Sally, who said she'd already put up a notice.

12.30: Texted Sally to ask how English Language Paper 2 went. She texted back: 'Fine. A big improvement on Rosabel. Go to sleep. Take paracetamol. Eat biscuits.'

2.15: Texted Sally to say the box of spare reading books for Year 8 was in the prison cupboard. Sally texted back: 'Go. Away. Get. Better.'

Slept until Spouse came home with a bunch of roses and more Lemsip.

DIL organized the Littluns into sending a 'Get well soon, Grandma!' video message.

Slept again all evening. Now wide awake and writing this at midnight. Wondering where the girls I bullied are now. And how they are.

Monday 11 June

And how do you start the conversation, even if you do want to tell more truths and be more honest about yourself? 'Hey, I know you thought I was a nice person, but . . .'

Spent the weekend under the duvet, watching films and re-reading *The Diary of Adrain Mole*. Had phone call from daughters in Isleworth telling me to take the week off.

Ha ha.

Homemade lemon cheesecake delivered by Son and DIL. Auntie Google says citrus is good for colds, and Spouse not keen on cheesecake, so I ate it all.

This morning, Bathroom Scales said I'd lost a pound, despite the cheesecake. Or maybe a pound and a half. No, just a pound. Or, perhaps – hang on, wait – no, just the pound.

When I walked into the office, Sally looked surprised. Told her that apart from having enough catarrh on my lungs to glue together a broken wardrobe, I was fully recovered, thank you.

My desk, no surprise, was layered with work I'd set for the cover lessons on Friday. Took half an hour to sort.

Year 11 English exams over, so had a double period free to mark all the cover work. Found a new hiding place in a languages classroom where I couldn't be seen from the door. Frightened a Year 8 girl who ran in hoping to use her phone illegally. She sprang into the air when I said hello.

Handy, though. My purple pen was running out, so her punishment was a trip to the English office to fetch me another.

Camilla is back. Presumed she'd caught my cold, but she doesn't look as though she's had one.

Tuesday 12 June

Marion took the Tuesday briefing. Adrain was at a conference. Not a whiff of Ofsted, or even an off of Whiffsted. She thanked staff for all the hard work we'd done – and still were doing – to prepare exam pupils, gave space for a few notices, told us a funny story, and let us go early.

Year 8 are in groups, designing parody travel advertisements such as 'Camp at Your Local Dump' or 'Holiday by the Bins Outside Subway'. Took them to a computer room to create their PowerPoint presentations. Reminded them to use all the persuasive language methods employed in real adverts. 'You've got to sell those holidays,' I said.

Great atmosphere in the room, full of amusement, if chaotic, and at one point I had a mammoth coughing fit and Lynne had to supervise while I ran for water.

Then, ten minutes before the bell, Goater ruined another group's presentation by pulling out their computer's plug before they'd saved their work.

'But why?' I said to her outside the room.

'I don't know.' She rubbed at her eyes. 'They kept boasting theirs was better than ours.'

'That's no reason,' I said, and told her to come and see me at break.

She already had a detention in maths.

'Tomorrow, then. Without fail.'

Spoke to her maths teacher later. 'I don't understand her,' he said. 'She pushed a Year 7 girl aside in the corridor yesterday, and the girl nearly fell.'

Opened SIMS to record Goater's detention and found she's had five in the last fortnight. Emailed her Head of Year. She emailed back to say she'd already asked parents to come in.

Year 13 sat Paper 2 this afternoon. Saw Conor and Matt leaving school afterwards and asked how it went. Matt said, 'Miss, like, on results day, remember you, like, did your best with us.'

Wednesday 13 June

Coughed much of the night. Slept downstairs. Worse, Sodoffsted are coming tomorrow.

Was in the office, busy not missing my Year 13 double lesson, and Camilla burst in, capitalizing all over the place: 'Have You Read The Email?'

'No, I've been marking,' I said. 'What is it?'

But I knew.

She said the inspectors had called Adrain at 11. She looked pale and distracted, as though looking for something. 'Have you seen my bag?' she said.

I hadn't.

'I'd better find it.' Her top lip was sweaty.

'It'll be fine, Camilla. Don't let Ofsted panic you,' I said.

She looked at me, but wasn't really looking. 'I guess,' she said, and left.

Discovered in Year 12 lesson that Chloe and Gus Private are newly dating. She must have been waiting for him to become less Gus. I thought that at least they could keep the same surname if they married, then remembered they weren't actually called Private.

Adrain the Philanthropist once more declared the school open until 9 p.m. tonight so that we could plan.

The good news: we all have less planning than with Mucksted I and II because we're missing Year 11s and 13s.

The terrible news: as Jim pointed out, with fewer lessons happening, we're more likely to be observed.

Planned detailed *Tempest* lesson for Year 7 and a travel writing lesson for Year 8s in case I'm inspected, and photocopied half a copse ready for Year 12 on Friday.

Went home to a salad.

The sentence above is one of the most depressing written in the history of humankind.

One spot on the left of my chin today, one to the right, and one in the middle of my forehead, like a dot-to-dot of a perfect triangle. I noticed Goater joining them up with her eyes – or I thought she was – while she sat in my detention at break.

I'm all for symmetry, but please.

Thursday 14 June

Adrain found me at 7.30 a.m. in the office, in the way I'm *sure* the Queen sometimes wanders downstairs to chat to housemaids. When he appeared at the door, I dropped my doughnut on the desk and had to pretend it wasn't leaking jam on to my planner.

He had a request. Was there any chance I could collect some ex-Journos together and present *Beauchamp Matters* in a Key Stage 3 assembly tomorrow morning?

One that the inspectors could watch.

Could I make sure the Pupil Premium pupils were included?

He knew it was a lot to ask.

But.

Please. The magazine was such a good ambassador for the school.

He'd noted (aka Barbara had checked the timetable) that I had a free morning until Period 4 today to organize it. Then he dropped to his knees and kissed my feet, washing them with his grateful tears. Or at least he would have, had he stayed any longer.

When he'd gone, I told my doughnut, 'You are now officially comfort food.'

Told Sally about Adrain's request when she arrived and added, 'I don't remember saying yes, though.'

'But you've agreed.'

I looked at my hands. 'I'm shaking. And I've got this horrid tickly cough. What if I retch on stage?'

She said, 'Look, do you want me to help?'

I put up one (shaking) hand, like a (shaking) traffic officer. 'Oh no. No. I couldn't – you have your own troubles.'

'Will you please stop that keep-well-away stuff? Say it. You need me.'

I hesitated.

'Well?' she said.

'I need you,' I parroted. It felt odd to my tongue.

Sally is . . . I want to write awesome, but Lukas would laugh if he knew.

187

By lunchtime, we'd corralled all the Journos by either registration post, school email or lesson-visiting. We'd given them three questions to answer that would form the structure for a mini-speech each. Each a mini-speech. Not while eating a peach. And not on a beach.

I've just finished writing my own speech, and polished up a *Beauchamp Matter* SpowerPoint.

Sodoffsted didn't, sadly. Instead, a serious-looking inspector visited my Year 8s to watch them rehearse their parody travel adverts. He made notes on an iPad. But he laughed at the Subway group's suggestion that sleeping by bins meant you didn't have to go far to put the rubbish out and said, 'Fair point.'

He didn't scare me, though. Adrain's SURPRISE! assembly has dwarfed it all.

Jim's wife sent in Welsh cakes. She'd made them in the early hours, awake with menopausal insomnia. We tried not to look pleased his wife couldn't sleep.

Bought three packets of Soothers on the way home.

Friday 15 June

Ah well. Sleep's probably over-rated anyway. Maggie Thatcher slept only four hours a night and she managed a punishing workload, making enemies of all those miners and selling off the council housing stock.

Still, after the restless cough-cough night, my legs were weak as Sally and I climbed the stage steps with the Journos behind us. We stood in a line. Before us were the upturned faces of Key Stage 3, a posse of supervising teachers, Adrain Parkes, Marion, and two inspectors.

Hoped no one could see the Soothers bulge in my left cheek.

On the screen was the cover of *Beauchamp Matters*.

I pulled the microphone down so Samuel could reach it and he said, 'Welcome to our presentation of *Beauchamp Matters*.' He read a short pre-written introduction, but then began to ad-lib. I glanced at Sally, but she grinned. He was fluent, bright and funny. Of course.

He finished with, 'Beauchamp does matter. And if they hadn't let me stay in the club after half-term, I would have started a petition and organized a march.'

Keen applause.

Each Journo stepped forward to deliver the mini-speeches, explaining how they'd become involved, what their contribution had been and what they'd learned. Some were shy, and Betsy couldn't stop giggling, but they managed. Lukas, strutting across the stage like a male model, got whoop-whoops before he even began.

Then Sally read out the three winning mini-sagas, displayed on the screen with accompanying images.

My turn. I looked at my speech and sucked hard on the cough sweet. Couldn't see anything I'd written that hadn't been said, or implied, already. Folded the sheet and told the audience I had little to add except that watching the Journos team pull together had been a privilege. 'They've taught me much this year,' I said. 'Lessons I won't forget.' As I said the word 'forget', the cough sweet fell out of my mouth on to the stage.

As we left the hall, Marion Coles caught up with me. 'Fabulous,' she said. 'Adrian will be your new best friend.' She winked. 'I loved the comedy finish. Best assembly this year.'

'I planned the ending that way,' I said. 'Honest.'

Break duty was a come-down and would have been dull. But just before the bell a Year 10 boy opened a bottle of (illegal) fizzy drink, forgetting he'd carried it around all morning. Half a pint of fizzy orange covers a lot of corridor wall.

The inspectors observed my Year 12 language lesson. Thankfully, they didn't spot that Gus and Chloe were holding hands under the table. And when one of the class mentioned Chinglish, I managed to steer them off it.

'How did we do in assembly?' the Journos asked at lunchtime.

Said I would send personal emails to each of their parents to thank them for giving birth to their child, although I wouldn't phrase it exactly that way.

Senior Writing Club is now officially renamed Journos Plus.

Went to local amateur theatre tonight with Spouse to see a depressing play about poor Irish people with dirty faces. The evening was lifted only by the interval's toffee fudge ice cream, although it tasted funny combined with the eucalyptus in the Soothers.

Monday 18 June

'Four weeks left,' I said to Mirror, 'and four spots to match. You're excelling yourself.'

'Are you getting on the scales?' it said. Sly as a draught under a door, that Mirror.

'I've been ill,' I said. 'You have to feed a cold.'

'Not for three,' it said.

Emergency briefing before registration. The official report wasn't out yet, Adrain said, so we must keep schtum. But Sodoffsted had pronounced us 'Good' in all aspects.

We clapped ourselves.

He was wearing a bright pink daisy-patterned tie today. And designer stubble on his chin, which is a new one on us. As I passed him, he said, 'Marvellous assembly. Thank you.'

'No worries,' I said, forgetting that Thou Shalt Not Lie.

At break time, giant chocolate cookies arrived in the staffroom with a thank-you card from the Smuts.

Discovered a box of Maltesers on my desk later. 'These from you?' I asked Sally.

'No.'

Camilla came in. She looked embarrassed. 'You found them.'

Difficult few seconds. Sally had spotted *Hamlet* on my desk while I took Camilla's revision classes and I'd had to tell her the reason. But Camilla didn't know that.

'Fabulous,' I said, slitting the wrapper with scissors. 'Shall we share them?'

'Not for me,' Camilla said. Her voice was flat, as though she was too tired to talk. She turned to leave, and I noticed she'd had to put a safety pin in the waistband of her skirt.

When she'd gone, Sally said, 'That was really nice of you, though, to take her classes.'

'It wasn't niceness.'

She shook her head. 'You're a weird one,' she said. 'But I'll forgive you, because you spat out a sweet on stage.'

Played Year 7 a *Tempest* film clip with Helen Mirren as Prospera, a female Prospero. They were outraged. 'Shakespeare would *not* be happy,' said one girl.

But they laughed like drains at Russell Brand's performance as the drunken Trinculo.

Showed the class a *Guardian* review that thought Mirren excellent and Russell Brand 'unfunny'. Discussion followed about interpretation, subjective opinion and the nature of art.

Lynne stayed behind afterwards. 'You taught them like sixth-formers. They loved it.'

Where are Sodoffsted when you need them?

Today's lesson had confirmed Lynne's decision, she said. She wanted to teach English.

I put my hands up. 'Whoa! Don't pin it on me when your family and friends forget your name.'

She thanked me for the morale boost.

Bahlul said after school, 'Looks like this Key Stage 4 work audit is never going to happen, doesn't it? Has Camilla forgotten?'

'And all that prep you've done on your Year 10 books', I said, 'gone to waste.'

Tuesday 19 June

Two spots are fading. The other two are on my forehead, plotting their next move.

Bathroom Scales said I'd stayed the same weight, and good for me. I said I didn't want to be the same weight. I wanted to be size 6.

'Realism is not in her skill set,' Mirror said.

Was asked to cover Sally's Year 8s in Period 3 as she had an appointment. She'd set them a test, so they were mostly cooperative. Browsed through a copy of *Beauchamp Matters* in her classroom. Re-read Leon's piece on abridged novels, caretaker George's funny interview, Paul Vinnicombe's description of his trapeze days, the debate on fast food, James's top ten scientists, and Betsy's hilarious opinion piece about the perils of dating schoolfriends. Felt like a mother with a new baby who thinks, 'Did I make that?'

Noora's bullying article sparked a conversation in the office later, while we waited for Camilla to arrive for the department meeting.

Jim said. 'It's as though Noora really got into the mind of the bully. Very mature and compassionate writing.'

Sally, back from her appointment, agreed.

'Noora should have interviewed me,' Jim said. 'I was a little terror at school.'

We all said, 'What?'

But then Camilla came in. No top tips. She had our draft timetables for next year.

Strange. She gave Bahlul his and he said, 'Oh.'

'What's up, mate?' Jim said. 'Expecting your P45?'

Bahlul squirmed and Camilla looked uncomfortable too. I saw Jim blush scarlet.

Spouse has found himself a book of Celtic prayers. Caught him reciting one in the kitchen while pouring wine. 'Grant to me rest. Grant to me rest,' he kept saying.

'Are you talking to God or the wine?' I said.

'Both.'

'Anyway, can I have one?'

He turned to me and chanted, 'Grant to me rest. Grant to me –'

'Oh, ha ha.'

Showed Spouse my draft timetable. Same old, same old. More GCSE and A-level teaching next year, though. He said, 'Even more marking.'

'Fewer reports, though.'

He said I wasn't selling it to him.

Wednesday 20 June

Camilla asked today if I had resources on *Jekyll and Hyde* for Year 10. She'd meant to plan last night but felt ill. Gave her a clutch of papers from my file. 'Thank you *so* much,' she kept saying.

Took Year 12 to the library for research on language investigation coursework. 'Well, this is interesting,' one said, looking round, much as Columbus did on landing in the Americas. (Not you, Privates.)

Gus and Chloe sat welded thigh to thigh, leafing through the same book, though their investigations are on different subjects.

'Should I go to Slimming World?' I asked Spouse this evening as he laced up his trainers.

'Come for a walk with me instead. It's free.'

'What about this Shakespeare scheme of work Camilla's asked me to write for next year?' I said.

'For. Next. Year,' he said. 'Come on. Get your trainers on.'

We walked across the field near our house. The sun spied on us from behind clouds.

It was my foster mother's birthday today. My own mum would have been seventy-two now. Surely thirty-one is too young to die by your own hand. Maybe cruelty had exhausted her. Tired of being treated cruelly. Tired of treating others cruelly. Tired of being cruel to herself. Which was which? The boundaries seem blurred.

'She often left you with neighbours when you were small,' Gran used to tell me. 'When she couldn't take you any more. Remember she was only a teenager.'

'What do you mean?' I'd say. 'What neighbours? How often?'

But then she'd lock up her lips as though afraid that secrets would slide out. And now she's dead too.

What did that look like? Not able to *take* me? I have no one to ask. Does it look like the messy, untreated scars that I can still trace, decades later, on the soft part under my left arm and on my thigh? Or the way that, in restaurants or pubs or at parties, I need to sit where I can see everyone, and not where they're behind me, perhaps a threat? Does it look like the child on the psychologist's film?

Bible study tonight focused on looking forward and pressing on, not looking back or letting your past dictate your future. My, my, I'm doing brilliantly on that score.

Thursday 21 June

Email from Adrain. *Beauchamp Matters* gets a special mention in the draft Ofsted report he's been sent. So does my Year 8 'parody advert' lesson.

Jim told me at break that the Smuts have hauled Bahlul in to discuss capability procedures. 'Ofsted noticed a discrepancy between his class's books and all of ours,' he said. 'And between his preparation and ours. Did you know that?'

I didn't. 'That explains the awkward timetable moment yesterday.'

'I wanted the earth to swallow me up,' he said.

'You weren't to know,' I said. 'Anyway, they can't sack him, surely?'

'He's tested their patience,' he said.

Years 7 and 12 reports both due in soon, Year 7 first. Started writing them this morning. Sally was writing hers too. She said, 'How can I say "won't shut up" but kindly?'

I'd had the same dilemma. 'I've put "articulate but needs to judge the moment" for one of mine.'

'That is genius. What about "handwriting is near illegible"?'

'"Clearly heading for medical profession"?' I said.

She squawked. 'You haven't put that!'

No, I hadn't.

'I'd forgotten you were a medical secretary,' she said. 'You'd know all about terrible handwriting.'

Camilla came in while we were yelping with laughter thinking up euphemisms for 'pokes schoolmates with compasses' or 'puts head on desk and snores in Period 5'.

We fell quiet, but she just said 'hi' in a nobody's voice, fetched a book and left.

'How are you and Archie?' I asked Sally as we packed up for the day.

'I can't really talk about it,' she said, 'or I'll be standing in a puddle of my own tears. The reports have helped me forget.'

Oh.

Saw the last of the Year 8 advert presentations today. Gave Leon's group merits for the best advert: 'Sun Yourself at the Sewage Works'. He'd written a rap:

Enjoy that stink
Breathe in the air
Beaches and bikinis
are so last year.

Friday 22 June

Rebekah turned up at the office before school began. I was there alone.

'I've finished all my exams, Miss,' she said. She'd brought back a borrowed tome on dystopian fiction. She said she needed three A-stars for her place at Cambridge to read English.

'I have total faith in you,' I said. No! Word association!

'Talking about faith,' she said, 'I still need to try your church.'

I suggested she visit us on Sunday.

In the Year 7 class, Zak's eyes were red and puffy. Angel Child gazed at me like a baby seal, as though begging me to help.

Told the class to continue their descriptions of the *Tempest* goddesses quietly if they wanted to escape the fires of hell (or something like that), left Lynne in charge, and spoke to Zak in the corridor.

'Is this about your exam result, Zak?' I said. 'You took the paper home to re-do, didn't you? Are you upset about that?'

'My mum's got liver disease,' he said. 'I think it's called squeerosis. Her face is yellow.' He rubbed his eyes.

'She's having treatment, I'm sure.'

'She says she won't die from it. Not – not soon.'

'They've caught it early. That's good news, Zak,' I said.

Asked if he was happy to come back into class. He was. I couldn't believe I'd said, 'That's good news, Zak.'

Emailed his form tutor in case she didn't know. She did. 'His foster parents are super,' she wrote back. 'That will make all the difference for him.'

Not true. It will make *some* difference.

Journos Plus was fun. Took inspiration from Year 8 lessons and they wrote parody fairy tales. 'These are hilarious,' I said when they'd read them out.

'Why don't we do parody fairy tales for next year's magazine competition?' they suggested.

How do I tell them?

When I got home, Spouse said, 'We're still on for Isleworth this weekend, aren't we? To see Mum and the girls?'

'Oops.'

'What?'

'Oh, nothing,' I said, thinking millstones.

Monday 25 June

Bathroom Scales this morning said I'd gained two pounds over the weekend.

'That's OlderDaughter's cooking,' I said. 'I can't say no to seconds. And thirds.'

Mirror said, 'You do an "n" and then an "o". What's so difficult?'

This weekend was the second time this year we've left the cooler Midlands for west London only to see temperatures leap.

Finished my Year 7 reports in Isleworth but didn't have time for Year 12's. I partly blame the World Cup and England's 6–1 win over Panama. It would have been letting the country down not to watch. And it was too hot to think.

'I should hope not, anyway,' said YoungerDaughter. 'Surely you're winding down at school now. Write the reports there.'

Told her there was no winding down involved. 'We plan for next year's teaching. Write new schemes of work. Update old ones. Evaluate the exam classes. Devise lesson plans. Research. Read. Focus properly on younger classes. Plus, I still have my Year 12s.'

She thanked me for the list and asked why I didn't go part-time.

Spouse said later, 'She's right.'

I replied, 'I'd be letting people down. It would feel as though I'd failed. Or it would prove that I couldn't take the strain.'

'What's wrong with that? You're not an ox.'

Texted a church friend while travelling home. 'Did a teenager visit this morning? Glasses. Dark hair.'

No. No visitors.

Goater is on Year 8 report. She has a card I have to sign after lessons to record her behaviour. Today she was on her best.

Watched a *Tempest* scene with Year 7 in which Stephano and Trinculo get distracted from the plot to murder Prospero by stumbling across a hoard of gaudy clothes they want to try on.

One girl called out, 'Miss! I am *so* the same in Primark.'

Zak seemed happier today. I'd re-marked his exam: 50 per cent. 'Onwards and upwards,' I said. And when I remembered to ask how Spain had gone, he looked like the old Zak.

Tuesday 26 June

We gathered at lunchtime for the department meeting, but Camilla wasn't there. While we waited, Bahlul confessed that the Smuts will start capability procedures if he doesn't play ball for the rest of the term.

'What does playing ball look like?' I said.

'Planning my lessons. Setting proper homework. Keeping to the department schemes of work. Meeting report deadlines.'

Jim said, 'Marking?'

And that, Bahlul admitted, his face woeful.

'You've described the entire job,' Jim said.

'I don't want to stop teaching,' Bahlul said, 'but I have no life.'

'You've described the entire job,' Jim said.

The office phone rang. Sally answered. 'That was Reception about Camilla. She had to go home.'

'Bonus,' said Bahlul.

Sally put the phone down and said, 'I think you mean, "Oh dear, I hope Camilla's OK."'

'Some extra marking time for you, Bahlul,' Jim said. He stood up. 'Meanwhile, I didn't get time for pudding.'

I went with Jim, even though my conscience was nagging me to start Year 12 reports. We left Bahlul bent over his desk, sighing like the wind.

Asked Jim over tepid apple crumble what he'd meant about being a terror at school.

'You don't want to know,' he said.

'But I do.'

He put his spoon down. 'I'm embarrassed.'

I waited.

'I learned it from my dad,' he said at last, 'although I didn't realize that at the time. He lost a leg from cancer as a young man and – well – when you feel powerless, being cruel to someone else, someone smaller, can help.'

I said, 'Oh.'

'And it's true. It can help,' he said.

'Can it?'

He met my eyes and I looked away. 'Yes,' he said. 'For a short while. After that, it screws you up. I've been in therapy for years to try and make me a decent bloke.'

'But you are –'

'Correction. To try and make me *feel* I'm a decent bloke.'

Wednesday 27 June

Apart from my Year 12 class, had a free day. If I hadn't covered a Camilla lesson, found a Year 9 girl crying in a corridor, listened to Bahlul's woes (again), discovered an error running through my Year 7 reports, re-planned tomorrow's Year 8 lesson on a whim, and photocopied the wrong side of a resource fifty times, I'd have started the Shakespeare scheme or written Year 12's reports.

Brought Year 12 some examples of language investigation projects. 'This one's about Beyoncé,' Olivia said. 'How did it deserve such a good mark?'

Ah, bless the Privates and their narrow perspectives.

'Look more closely, Olivia,' I said. 'It's about the use of semantic fields in media reportage about Beyoncé. It's well researched, comprehensive and discusses linguistics at a high level.'

'You mean, it's not about her twerking,' someone else said.

One boy leafed through a language investigation as though it were a holy text and breathed, 'This must have taken a lot of hard work.'

'Yes,' I said. 'Welcome to the next six months of your life.'

At Bible study tonight, the God-lady wished we had more young people in the church. 'We are mainly over fifties,' she said.

I thought that for someone born just after the Great Flood, that was an understatement.

'It would be lovely', she said, 'to see some younger Christians joining us.'

I buried my head deep in a piece of ginger cake.

Thursday 28 June

Am currently ignoring Bathroom Scales. 'Don't be offended,' I said. 'You were just doing your job, I know.'

'Are you ignoring me too?' Mirror wanted to know.

'I would like nothing more,' I said, peering closer. 'Would you say my nose is redder than it was?'

'Does she mean the Baileys?' Mirror said to Bathroom Scales.

Bathroom Scales kept quiet. A painful, spurned silence.

Year 8 are now studying the writings of nineteenth-century female explorers. Today: Isabella Bird. 'Remember, no one had TV in those days,' I said. 'Or the internet. We relied on people like Isabella Bird to describe the places they were exploring. Otherwise, how would we know?'

Challenged them to write a description of the school dining hall for an alien who had never visited earth. One boy described chips. He wrote, 'They are made of potato. They are long and thin and fried. Fried means boiled in oil. They go with tomato ketchup . . .'

'Could you describe the surroundings too?' I suggested. 'The walls? The tables? The tall windows?'

'Hang on, Miss.' He stalled me with a hand. 'Just thinking how to describe ketchup.'

Babysat for Son and DIL tonight while they went out for a curry. Took Year 12 report-writing with me. But Son and DIL have Netflix.

Friday 29 June

Not sure what was wrong with Years 7 and 9 today, but in both lessons I felt I'd lost control. World Cup fever is a factor, but that can't explain everything.

I had three Year 7s and two Year 9s with me during break duty and not for a social occasion. 'Line up against the wall,' I said.

'Are you going to shoot us?' asked one of the Year 9 boys.

'No,' I said, 'but you're going to watch me eat this flapjack.'

'Shoot us, shoot us. Quick!' he said, and the others giggled.

It's hard to punish the funny.

Goater still on report. Am trying to praise her more. I'm parsimonious with praise compared to Sally, who doles out stickers and congratulations from a bottomless pit of goodwill. But it works with Goater. 'All these good comments from teachers!' I said today, signing her report. 'You must be trying so hard.' She blushed, but her eyes thanked me.

Journos Plus and I have a bond now, forged in the fire of *Beauchamp Matters*. I wonder if the people at the *Daily Mail* or *The Times* feel the same. We wrote poems today and Noora penned one about bullies. I'm copying it here to preserve it.

They eat breakfast like others.
Weetabix. Shreddies. Toast with jam.
They go to school like others.
Bus. Train. Legs.
They wear uniform like others.
Tie. Shirt. Black Shoes.
They sit through lessons like others.
Geography. History. Maths.

But when their blood is up
or someone has riled them
or something has made them small
they do not act like others
but like the monstrous
breathing out the fire that
someone else has coughed into them.

Lukas was away, though, perhaps recovering from England's loss to Belgium yesterday.

Spouse said a minute ago, 'What are you writing?'

I explained. He asked me to read it out. When I had, he said, 'Wow.'

'I'm going to find her some poetry competitions,' I said.

'Good, but why are you writing it out in your diary?'

I nearly said. I *nearly* said.

Monday 2 July

Went to Son and DIL's for lunch after church yesterday. Asked DIL if she'd come to Slimming World. She's talked about wanting to lose weight. We looked up our most local group while waiting for Son to carve the roast. Monday evenings, 6.30.

'What?' I said. 'That's tomorrow.'

'And we've brownies and fudge ice cream for dessert,' she said. 'Maybe we should skip that.'

But even violent criminals get the choice of a last meal, and what's good enough for axe murderers is good enough for me.

Camilla was back in today. She is a different Camilla from autumn-term Camilla, like the sketch drawing of a portrait instead of the painted version. Jim is solicitous, almost like a father. 'Did you get a coffee at break, Camilla?' 'I've got this great lesson I did with Year 9. Would you like a copy?' 'Would you like half of my Twix?'

Feel I've avoided Jim since our conversation over apple crumble. I know I wasn't honest, pushing him to share his troubles but holding tight to mine.

Year 8 made predictions today about *The Tempest*. Would Prospero forgive his enemies by the end of the play? If not, what would he do? They had gruesome ideas for Prospero's disposal of his enemies. I suspect their screen diet is not *Antiques Roadshow* and *Countryfile*.

Goater has been taken off report now that her behaviour has improved. 'I am so pleased,' I said, when she told me. She did tut when a classmate called Prospero's brother Antonia instead of Antonio, but, tiny steps.

Pressed Send on my Year 7 reports, feeling smug, then SIMS crashed. SIMS and Bahlul should get together. They both prefer not working to working.

Got a shock on the scales at Flab Club. I took off my watch, my earrings, my shoes and my cardigan before stepping on, and breathed in. But even so . . .

'Don't say it out loud,' I said to the woman supervising the weighing.

'I wouldn't,' she said. 'We write it in your book, silently.'

'Now you're making it sound like a dirty secret,' I said.

She looked at me as if thinking, *This one's going to be tough work.*

DIL has less to lose than I do. But that's not hard.

Tuesday 3 July

In staff briefing, Adrain said that the official Ofsted report should be publicly available any day. He delivered the news as though he thought we'd all been losing sleep over it since the inspection. Staff are more buzzed about the Beauchamp School World Cup sweepstake.

SIMS came back to life this morning, but my Year 7 reports had disappeared. Spent Period 4 copying and pasting them all back in. This is why I took a postgraduate teaching degree, to train me for the copying and pasting. The photocopying. The stapling. The hole-punching.

Bahlul wasn't at the department meeting, though we knew he was in school. Camilla said he had 'an appointment', but Jim told me and Sally afterwards that he was with Marion and Colin, learning more about how to play ball.

'He's definitely doing more marking,' I said. 'He keeps stealing purple pens from my stationery drawer.'

Had tuna salad and a baked potato in the dining room. 'I'm getting some sticky toffee pudding and custard,' Jim said. 'Want some?'

I said, 'Desperately, with all my heart, and more than you could possibly know,' and told him about Slimming World.

He said, 'Do you want me to sit at another table and eat mine?'

I said, 'Of course not,' and while he tucked in I faked enjoyment of a satsuma.

I feel sorry for Camilla – so much so that I asked Year 12 whether they'd changed their mind about sitting in shapes yet. They hadn't, but I told her that I'd asked.

'Oh,' she said in a whisper. A wisp of a whisper.

Found Year 12 some World Cup reports in Indian English, Chinese English and British English to compare. 'Don't say I never give you anything,' I said to the football-mad contingent.

Sally says Archie is trying to kick his gambling addiction.

'Is he getting professional help?' I asked.

'He thinks he can do it on his own,' she said, but her voice had a tremor.

Wednesday 4 July

Bathroom Scales said I'd lost a pound. Told them a pound wasn't enough. 'I'm using up masses of emotional energy resisting treats. Are you sure that's all?'

They were sure.

DIL messaged me. She's lost three.

Paul Vinnicombe peered round my classroom door in Period 3 today to say that his street cred had shot up. He said the kids were behaving better for him now and he wishes he'd mentioned his circus experience the first day he started at Beauchamp.

I bet he does. He's been at the school five years.

He also said he's persuaded Adrain to let him book a circus skills troupe for an afternoon with Year 10 next year.

'Will you be wearing a leotard?' I said.

'You wish,' he said.

Some of Year 12 are recording spoken data for their investigations, so today they practised transcribing speech into written form.

'Remember the conventions for transcriptions,' I said. 'Write down what you hear, and indicate pauses and overlaps the way I've shown you. But no commas, question marks, full stops. Nothing. Not even capital letters.'

'No capitals or punctuation?' one boy said. He punched the air and said he'd been rehearsing for this day since primary school.

Sally had brought in a sparkly blue dress and glittery shoes, as she was going straight to the Year 11 prom from school. She hung the dress on the back of the office door. 'Why aren't you coming?' she said.

'First,' I said, 'I don't have anything in my wardrobe suitable, and, second, I am not into ritual humiliation in front of Year 11s.'

She asked if I meant dancing.

'I do.'

'C'mon,' she laughed. 'What are you ashamed of?'

I wasn't sure what to say. I turned to my desk and tidied some already-tidy papers.

'Have I upset you?' she said after a while.

There was a hard lump of something in my throat, stopping words.

'I wish you were coming,' she said. 'We could have had a chat. We don't get time to talk properly at school.'

At home, Spouse had bought me some cans of gin and slimline tonic. Had one before Bible study and then another one afterwards so that no one can say my life lacks balance.

Thursday 5 July

I had a night sweat, but I don't know if it was the menopause or the summer or the gins. Auntie Google couldn't decide. Either way, I woke all slippery, like a cod.

At school, was uploading Year 12 reports when Sally walked into the office. She said the police were called to the prom yesterday to haul away a gatecrashing posse of teenagers. And then an ambulance came because Danny had mistaken the dance floor for a rugby pitch and play-tackled another boy. 'He broke his shoulder,' she said.

'Who – the boy did?'

'No, Danny. The boy moved out of the way. Danny crashed to the floor.'

I said it was a shame the evening had been spoiled.

'On the contrary,' she said. 'Year 11 said it all made up for the buffet. And the paramedics ripped Danny's shirt off, which gave everyone a treat.'

'Was the buffet that bad?' I said.

'Curly egg sandwiches, and sausage rolls that had never seen a pig.'

I said I'd been right not to come. Sausage rolls weren't part of the Slimming World regime.

'You're going to Slimming World? You didn't say. Although – there's a lot you don't say.'

I told her I'd had a very quiet evening in comparison to hers, at a Bible study about the gifts of the Holy Spirit.

She frowned. 'I didn't understand a word you just said. What happens at a Bible study? What kind of gifts?'

'OK, so . . .' I tried to explain.

God-lady would be proud.

Gave Year 8 an extract from *Notes from a Small Island* by Bill Bryson as an example of humorous travel writing. Leon said, 'Why haven't you shown us this before?' He said he would download some of Bryson's books.

'Download?' I said.

His mum has bought him a Kindle as she's so pleased with his reading.

Bill, I hope you appreciate the spike in sales. Feel free to send a share of your royalties.

Had a yawning fit on the bus on the way home. Once I start, I can't stop. The man next to me started yawning too. 'You're infectious,' he said loudly, and all the other passengers looked round.

Friday 6 July

We've mislaid Camilla. 'She disappeared Period 4 yesterday,' Sally told me this morning. 'Raced into the office, rummaged in a drawer, then left again.'

'Rummaged for what?'

'Some kind of medication. Pill bottle. She tucked it away pretty sharpish.'

'Maybe she'll be in later,' I said.

But she wasn't.

The Ofsted report is out. 'You've got two mentions, you jammy woman,' Jim said to me.

'I've got a mention too,' Bahlul said, so we asked him where. He pointed to where the inspectors had written that the vast majority of the teaching in the English department was praiseworthy. He said, 'I'm in the bit between the lines.'

'Ouch,' Sally said.

'Why do you think Marion's office is my second home these days?' he said.

'Lucky you!' Jim said.

Sally nudged me, hard.

Here's a thing. Bahlul is clearly a substandard teacher as far as professional standards go. None of us are sure he'll ever be anything but a substandard teacher. We even cover for him being substandard at times.

Bahlul knows he's a substandard teacher.

But he's still part of the team.

And at least Bahlul isn't hiding it, stacking piles of unmarked exercise books in a dark cupboard or disguising the fact that he's in major trouble with the Smuts.

Goater looked pale today. I asked her if something was wrong. She stayed after the bell to tell me her mum had left the family home.

'I'm so sorry,' I said.

She said that her dad had been in school this morning, talking to her Head of Year. 'Mum's living in France with a – with a friend.'

How did Goater feel about that?

'We get on, me and Dad,' she said. 'He's – kind of lighter on me. I will miss my mum, but . . .'

At home, Spouse keeps dragging his trousers up, like Compo on *Last of the Summer Wine*. Asked him to give the powerspeeding a break in case he loses more weight. It's embarrassing that the one going to Slimming World is hardly losing anything and the one not going is about to slip down a drain.

'It's part of my life now,' he said. 'But why not come? You enjoyed it last time. It'll help with the weight loss.'

So we had a chicken salad at home, then walked across the field to the pub next to the river. We sat outside with glasses of red wine, watching the sun dip down and more down.

'I've got Year 8 books to mark and Year 12 essays,' I said, 'but I'm finding it hard to care.'

Spouse patted me on the back.

Monday 9 July

Rebekah didn't show up at church yesterday. I felt relieved, then guilty for being relieved. Guilty relieved guilty relieved guilty guilty guilty.

Survived worship-leading, except I kicked off a quiet, thoughtful song two keys too low. Startled everyone out of their reverie with,

'Oops. Hang on. I'll whack that up.' God-lady sat down with a thump. I don't think it takes much at her age.

The sermon was about gratefulness. 'What are you thankful for?' the preacher said.

(You not being here, Rebekah.)

Glad preachers can't see into minds. The day Derren Brown joins the church and goes on the preaching rota, I'm going over to the Quakers.

Year 7 wrote hyperbolic opinions today about how *The Tempest* ends. Skimmed through their books after the lesson. They're still convinced Prospero should have done unspeakable things to his enemies rather than forgive them, especially his brother, Antonio. The theme of forgiveness seems to have passed them by.

Lost three pounds at Flab Club. DIL lost four. She hugged me.

'Steady on,' I said. 'There's a way to go yet before I can wear jeans without elastane.'

Spouse said when I got home, 'See? That walk on Friday night did you good.'

'Hey, I know your game,' I said.

I watched a nature programme tonight in which tigers chased down young deer, leapt on to their necks and brought them to the ground with a bite. It seemed cruel. Spouse said it wasn't cruel – it was instinctive behaviour. Their parents teach them the way of the predator, and they are wired like that. 'There's no malice in it. That's how they are. They don't know another way.'

Tuesday 10 July

In briefing, Adrain announced, sadly, that Pam is retiring on ill health grounds.

Oh. So Camilla –

'But Camilla isn't coming back either,' he added. He said Barbara was drafting the advertisement today.

Sally glanced at me. I knew we were both thinking, *Who's going to be free to start a September Head of Department post when they'd have to give half a term's notice?*

Back in the department office, we found Camilla had emailed each of us. 'Is your message the same as mine?' Sally said. 'She has an anxiety disorder?'

'Yes.' But it wasn't quite the same. At the end of mine, Camilla had added her mobile number and asked me to call.

At break, I closed my classroom door and dialled her number.

'Is anyone else in the room?' Camilla asked. She sounded as though she'd been crying.

'No. On my own in here.'

'Can I tell you something?' she said. 'I feel I should explain.'

'You don't have to,' I said.

'I want to.'

She told me she'd become dependent on painkillers, drugs prescribed after her accident. Now, she couldn't get through a day without them. 'I won't go into the gory details. But I've started having terrifying panic attacks,' she said. She'd moved back in with her parents. 'Although I don't know why. They didn't exactly cover themselves in glory when I was small.'

'I'm sorry.'

'And my GP is suggesting talking therapies. Maybe even rehab if I can't kick the pills that way.'

I said I was glad she was getting help.

She said, 'Look, please don't tell the others all this.'

I wanted to know why she was telling me.

'Because you've been so gracious. You've helped me. I was jealous, so I think I've been a cow to you particularly. Sometimes deliberately.'

Jealous? 'I haven't been more gracious than anyone else,' I said. 'What about all Jim's kindnesses?'

'I wasn't jealous of anyone else,' she said.

'But I don't understand why you'd be jealous.'

She said, 'You're everything I wish I was. As a teacher. As a person.'
I am? I didn't know what to say.

'You could have been a cow back,' she said. 'All that grief I gave you about the coursework. And the shaping. But you weren't.'

I had to say it. 'I've been nice to your face, Camilla.'

Pause.

'That's honest,' she said. 'But it makes no difference.'

'You agreed with the final coursework marks then,' I said, smiling with my voice.

'I sent them straight off,' she said, 'without even checking. I knew I could trust you.'

Checked emails tonight to find one from the *emagazine* editor. Did I have any other ideas for articles?

None whatsoever. My mind is as blank as a new canvas.

Wrote back saying that of course I had plenty of ideas. Brimming over with them. Would send some asap.

Sports Day tomorrow. My house colour is yellow. Am meant to wear a yellow T-shirt. 'I don't have one,' I told Sally today. 'And yellow makes my face look recently deceased.'

Have made myself a badge to wear on my blue T-shirt. It says, 'I am a yellow T-shirt.'

Wednesday 11 July

Walked to the sports field at 9 a.m., supervising untidy gaggles of pupils in their games kit. A warm day. The sun dodged behind clouds, then back out with a skip in its step, maybe influenced by World Cup fever like everyone else.

The T-shirt badge was a mistake. Pupils trying to get the joke had to stare at my chest for a good thirty seconds. I took the badge off.

Jim, Sally and I were put in charge of the rounders games. But apart from some light discipline from Jim ('If you throw those bats at people again, I will personally disembowel you') the kids were carefree in mood and happy to be not-in-maths. Two sixth-formers – sergeant majors or prison guards in waiting – took control.

We watched, seated on chairs stolen from the sports pavilion. A Year 7 slave fetched us tea in polystyrene cups.

'Anyone going for Camilla's job?' Jim said. But before we could say anything, he stood up and yelled, 'Oi! You! Yes, you! Try that trick again and you'll be sitting here, with us.'

He sat and turned to me. 'You've had a good year. You must be pleased.'

I started to demur.

'Oh, tell the truth,' said Sally. 'Ofsted loved you. The magazine was a triumph. You're a triumph.'

Tell the truth. 'It hasn't all been good,' I said.

Sally: 'Oh?'

I said, 'Everywhere I've looked this year I've been reminded of my childhood.'

They waited. I sipped my tea, not sure what to say next.

'Not in a good way,' Sally said.

'No.'

'Were you treated badly as a child?' she asked.

Jim said, 'This makes sense.'

I said I had, but I'd also treated others badly.

'You and me both, as I told you,' said Jim.

We all watched as a girl scored a rounder, and we clapped. I filled in a touch more detail. They listened without interrupting.

'Look, do I come over as a nice person?' I said. 'Tell me, honestly.' I swallowed.

Sally looked at Jim and said, 'What do we do with her?' She broke off to jog to the wicket and sort out an argument about batting.

Jim sighed. 'Look at that sunshine,' he said. 'It's a blessing.'

A blessing? 'That's not a very atheist word,' I said.

He said everyone had their off days, then, 'Sally says she's told you about the troubles she's having with her fiancé.'

I stayed quiet. How much did he know?

He continued, 'Gambling almost did for me once. I've given her the details of a charity that rescued me.'

I said that was helpful.

'Hm. Sadly I'm not convinced that her chap wants help.'

Missed the Croatia v England semi-final tonight because of Bible study and meant to catch up afterwards, but saw the result on Twitter. Just as well, maybe. Wasn't really in the mood.

Will write tomorrow about what happened in Bible study. Am not sure what to think.

Thursday 12 July

Spent most of today marking Year 12's practice transcriptions and their commentaries on them. Strange, putting ticks where there's no punctuation or capitalization, and writing, 'Well done. Accurate work.'

Taught Year 8. In the lesson, someone leaned over to Goater and told her she'd missed a question out. I saw her flush, but she said 'thanks' and began correcting her mistake.

Go, Goater!

So, last night's Bible study. We discussed Jesus' attitude to children. The leader asked us to share a happy memory from childhood. He gave us a minute to think.

I said it before I decided not to: 'I don't remember many happy things.'

A few laughed, then stopped. 'Oh. We thought you were joking. You usually are.'

They had suggestions. A birthday party? A Christmas present? A holiday? Surely . . .

They jogged my memory. 'I remember a toy vacuum cleaner Mum gave me for Christmas when I was seven. She left it wrapped at the end of my bed. But she wasn't pleased that I opened it before dawn and started vacuuming my bedroom. It made a racket.'

I thought back, remembering the injustice of it, that she'd bought a noisy present then yelled and flailed because I'd turned it on.

I said, 'She took it off me, then locked me back in the room.'

'Locked?' someone asked.

'She locked me in at night,' I said, 'I think so that she could go to town drinking and I'd be safe.'

They were silent. I heard someone whisper, 'Safe?'

'Sorry,' I said. 'It's depressing. In fact, I'm shocked saying it. I'm not sure I've ever told the story.'

Spouse said, 'You haven't. I didn't know this.'

God-lady said, 'Bless you, dear.'

Felt guilty. I'd made it difficult for the group. But also I felt lighter.

A rash of spots this morning, though, as if my face was also shocked. Life is so topsy-turvy at the moment, as though everything's flipped and I'm looking at things from the underneath.

I told a funny story to Bible study which wasn't funny. And we're out of the World Cup after all that thrill.

And Donald Trump has arrived in the UK today and will meet the Queen tomorrow.

Friday 13 July

Slept for six hours last night. Plus, Bathroom Scales are pleased with me, and my trousers are looser. I'm acclimatizing to my bread-less, cream-less, cake-less existence and it's paying off, even if I do salivate like a bloodhound when I pass a bakery.

One week until the end of term. Another new spot on the end of my nose. On break duty in the sunny corridor, I kept in the shade in case the sun lit the spot up like a beacon, and a confused ship foundered on the coast.

Last Journos Plus of the term. We wrote summer haiku and they ate strawberry laces. 'Will you all come back next year?' I said. I didn't mention the magazine. Maybe Adrain will find the money after all.

They'd signed a card for me. 'Sorry, Miss,' Noora said. 'We shouldn't have let James and Samuel organize it.' The two boys looked shy.

'Thank you, everyone,' I said. 'I like pictures of Second World War bombers anyway.'

Reached home at 7 p.m. and sent some ideas to the *emagazine* editor. She replied within minutes. 'These look really interesting. Will get back to you.' Someone else who works late, then.

Spouse went to Asda for mince on the way back from powerspeeding and returned with the mince and a bottle of Baileys Chocolat: a mix of Irish Cream and Belgian chocolate, new to both of us.

Told him about the editor's positive response. 'I'll celebrate that,' I said, 'to justify drinking liquid chocolate.'

He poured it into glasses. 'Also,' he said, 'you let your guard down at Bible study on Wednesday and lived.'

'Don't push it,' I said. 'I don't like being needy. I wish I hadn't said it.'

'But what are you afraid of? It was the truth.'

The truth. It's like a magician with a hundred scarves hidden inside a hat. Pull one out and along comes another. And another. And another. And another.

Monday 16 July

Went for a long walk with Spouse and the Littluns on Saturday. Videoed my feet (on purpose!) while I walked, then posted to Facebook for all the friends and family who'd forgotten I could move.

Have bought new trainers. Have also started reading a Rachel Joyce novel called *Perfect*. A kind of rebellion: reading for pleasure *before* the holidays begin. Why have I not found Rachel Joyce's writing before now?

Spouse said, 'Because you don't spend enough time looking?'

The Littluns hopped along behind us in the field, searching for sticks and leaves and telling us about school. Grandgirl told us someone pushed her over last week, so she went to the teacher.

'Good girl,' I said. 'If someone hurts you, always tell someone. Straight away.'

'OK,' she said. 'Will you carry my leaves in your pocket?'

After the walk, I sent a pitch to a parenting magazine for an article about the role of grandparents in teaching children to stay safe. Said to Spouse, 'If I have to get old, I may as well make a few bob out of it.'

He said that dropping the expression 'a few bob' might also help keep me young.

Mirror said to Bathroom Scales this morning, 'Don't let her get cocky, just because she's lost a few pounds.'

'Seriously, though.' I tested my face at different angles. 'Do you think my double chin is a bit less double?'

Mirror humphed.

We have no one leading our department for the final week. I'm organizing the Year 12s I shared with Camilla and we're managing other classes between us. We've sent Camilla a card and some flowers. Bahlul offered to sort Camilla's Year 7 work. Jim feigned a collapse.

'I'm up to date, pal,' Bahlul said, 'and so would you be if you'd been on Death Row.'

Saw George in the corridor. He's pleased. I'd placed his profile piece in the magazine alongside Colin's. 'I think I win in the personality stakes,' he said, grinning. 'We look like Laurel and Hardy.'

Two pounds off, according to the Slimming World scales. And DIL lost two as well. 'Snap,' she said, and high-fived me, which made me feel young and old all at once.

Spouse wanted to know this evening whether, as I'd enjoyed our walks, I'd also like to join in a meditation on a passage from Isaiah. Give him an inch.

'I have limits,' I said. 'Please, never ask me this again.'

Spent the evening writing grade reports in the study. The neighbours were having a barbecue. I could smell garlic and charcoaled fish and onions.

Tuesday 17 July

Another night sweat. Suddenly the duvet is an enemy to be fought off. It's like being lain on by a giant alpaca. Spouse trudged into the spare room to evade attack.

Today was School Activities Day. I've supervised pupils learning to flower-arrange, kick-box and street dance. I joined in with the flower-arranging.

My short story made it into the anthology for September publication! Told Sally in the office at break time. She said, 'What's the story about?'

'A woman gets an anonymous letter to say her husband's seeing someone else. So she –'

'No spoilers,' she said. 'I'll read it.'

'You will?'

'Of course.'

'Hey, don't tell Jim I asked you this,' she said. 'But, he and Marion – do you know anything? Are they . . .'

I shook my head. 'I only know what you know. That we don't know. I think I'm happier not knowing.'

'I guess.' She was opening a cake tin. 'Something else I was going to ask. You remember what you said at Sports Day about being cruel to younger children . . .' I didn't like hearing it from someone else's lips. It made it true. 'Is that why you became a teacher? To make up for it?'

She offered me lemon cake, but I waved it away, patting my stomach. 'You've become Camilla,' she said. 'You may as well take her job.'

I knew I ought to say that as a Christian I believed I was forgiven anyway. I shouldn't need to atone for my own sins. But that would have been only half true. Although I believed it, I clearly hadn't acted on that belief.

She got there first. 'Aren't you lot supposed to feel forgiven? You know, Jesus and all that.'

217

Told her she was right. 'But shame is like a limpet. Hard to shake off.'

She said, 'Jim told me his dad beat him daily. He learned cruelty that way. Then passed it on.'

The bell rang for lessons. 'Jim and I have a lot in common,' I said.

She said she thought so too and that she was going to leave the lemon cake on her desk in case I changed my mind later and Jesus wasn't enough.

'Oh, he will be,' I said, but she was on her way out and I don't think she heard.

Email from Adrain. Was I free to pop into his office tomorrow? Whatever time suited me.

I've decided I miss Tuesday afternoon coursework sessions with Year 13. I even miss Conor and, like, Matt.

After school, asked Sally whether she'd thought of applying for the Head of Department job. She said she hadn't. She'd have enough to cope with next year just being married to Archie. She made it sound like a trial.

Should I say it? 'Sally, do you think that – do you wonder whether –?'

'Don't,' she said, her eyes filling up. 'I know. I know already.'

Wednesday 18 July

Adrain was drawing his office blinds against a nosy sun when I arrived at break time. Marion was there too. My heart thumped. Was this about the non-shaping? Had Adrain discovered the misprint of his name? The lack of acknowledgements? My Year 12 Las Vegas comment?

I sat on the edge of a chair, my hands in my lap.

Marion said, smiling, 'We'll get to the point. We'd very much like you to apply for Head of English. In fact, we're happy to beg.'

My mouth dropped open like Marley's Ghost's in *A Christmas Carol*, when he undoes the head bandage keeping his jaw together.

Fortunately, Adrain and Marion seemed happy to continue while I gaped.

I'd impressed them with my work on the magazine, they said, and with the Pupil Premium Journos. Also, Camilla had sung my praises and I'd had two honourable mentions in the Ofsted report. 'And,' said Marion, 'the signs are that your exam classes will fly. As they have since you joined Beauchamp.'

'The advert went live yesterday,' Adrain said. 'We'll need to interview in the holidays. You'd be excellent.' He smoothed his hand over his head.

'But –'

'We fished out your CV.' Marion waved a sheet of paper. 'You've been Acting Deputy in a previous school. What's stopped you going further?'

Time for truth. Again. 'I've always preferred the classroom. Teaching, planning, making resources – it's what I do best. Management would take me away from that.'

'That can't be denied,' Marion said. Did I detect sadness? 'But please, think about it.'

Last lesson with Year 12. Poor attendance, as expected. But the Privates were there, demanding education. We studied holiday brochures and identified graphological features, which humoured them. Chloe had brought a giant box of Maltesers. For good measure, we analysed persuasive language on the box while we ate them.

This evening, told Bible study group about the Head of Department vacancy. God-lady said, 'Do you feel called to this?'

'I don't know,' I said. 'Something's calling me, but I'm not sure it's God.'

Jean asked how much more work it would entail.

Spouse said, 'Sore point.'

'I'd get paid more,' I said.

'We manage now,' he said.

The room went quiet. 'Think carefully, dear,' said God-lady. 'Make sure you're listening to the right voices.'

As we left, Jean told me she'd read *The Road*. 'Thank you for the recommendation,' she said.

'It wasn't too – er . . .'

'I made sure to read it in the daytime,' she said, patting my shoulder. 'Don't worry.'

Thursday 19 July

Had my hair cut yesterday after school. Said to Mirror this morning, 'It's even greyer now. Maybe I should dye it. Do you think I should dye it?'

Mirror said, 'Sometimes she wants my opinion. Sometimes she doesn't. So inconsistent.'

Bathroom Scales said, 'To be honest, she's the same with me.'

It's happened. They have joined forces.

Last lesson with Year 8. I ditched the seating plan and they leapt into friendship groups. Goater looked unsure where to settle.

'Over here,' another girl called. 'Come sit with us.' She tapped the seat beside her. The mercy of it constricted my throat and I didn't have the heart to tell the girl it was 'Come *and* sit' and that we weren't in New York.

I'd compiled a 'literary terms' crossword, which they completed good-naturedly while crunching lollipops. 'Soliloquy' caused an issue, though. They felt its inclusion a gross injustice.

Leon announced that he'd found a book of Shakespeare stories in the library written by someone called Leon.

'Leon Garfield!' I said. 'Of course. He wrote *Smith* as well, didn't he?'

'Downloaded that yesterday,' he said, looking proud.

Was in the office packing up my summer reading – Thomas Hardy for next year's sixth-formers, a new English Language textbook, a copy of *Othello* for Year 10 – when Rebekah knocked.

'You can't keep away,' I said.

She said it was true. She missed school. 'I need to prepare for uni. Do you have any literary criticism or history of literature I can borrow?'

'They'll send a reading list – you know that?'

'Yes, but I want to start now.'

'Sorry. Nothing left,' I said. 'Conor and Matt got here before you.' It took her a few seconds to get the joke.

We browsed the shelves and she loaded up her bag. 'I'll bring it all back in September,' she said.

'I know you will.'

'Oh,' she said. 'About church.'

I waited.

'I found somewhere,' she said. 'In Kenilworth. Someone in my form has admitted to being a Christian and she took me. I might play in the band.'

I said I was delighted for her. (And for me, Rebekah.)

'But why do people wait so long to own up?' she said.

This evening, walked with Spouse over the fields to the pub and talked truth until the sky went flame then pink then grey. I told him about the first-year pupils at my school all those years ago and how I'd treated them. 'Sorry I haven't told you,' I said. 'I was ashamed.'

He topped up my wine.

'Do you think I bully *you*?' I asked him.

'Wouldn't I have noticed by now?'

'But what if you've got used to it over the years and think it's normal?' I said.

He looked at me. 'Like you had to, you mean?'

I stood up and walked towards the river, so I wasn't facing him. 'Do you think I should go for therapy or something?'

'Do you?'

I said I didn't know. And I don't.

221

Friday 20 July

Told Mirror, 'It's my last day. Be nice.'

'OK,' it said. 'You have no spots.'

'Yes, I do,' I said, leaning in.

'You asked me to be nice, so I lied.'

Bathroom Scales tittered. 'She asked for that.'

Ladyshave said, 'Fickle or what?'

Met Marion and Adrain before school to say I wouldn't apply for Head of English . . .

'Now, that's a shame,' Adrain said.

. . . But would like to switch to part-time teaching from January.

'Ouch,' Marion said. 'Right hook. Then left hook.'

'We weren't prepared for that,' Adrain mansplained. Mansplained Adrain.

Told them my reasons.

They said that they didn't want to lose me. 'We'll look at staffing and try our best,' Marion said. 'I'm sure we can sort something out.'

As I closed the door, I heard Marion say, 'OK, so it's Plan B.'

Someone said, 'Pssst.' It was Adrain's secretary, Barbara, beckoning me to her tiny office. She said, 'You saw my typo, I suppose? Adrian's name? I wasn't going to confess, but –'

'So it wasn't me?' I said.

She giggled. 'A drain!' She put her hand over her mouth. 'A drain!'

In the office, I told Jim and Sally that I'd requested part-time, but not about the Head of Department offer. 'You won't know yourself,' Jim said.

'It's so right for you,' Sally said, and hugged me.

Year 7's last lesson. First, I gave back their essays and explained the concept of forgiveness. Second, a *Tempest* quiz and Jelly Babies to toast Ferdinand and Miranda's future dynasty.

Zak said, 'My foster parents writ you a note in my planner.' He foraged in his bag.

The note read, 'Thank you for supporting Zak. He loves your lessons.'

Gave Lynne a David Crystal book. She bowed and said, 'O blessed be his holy name.'

My final lesson of the year was with Jim's Year 9s. Jim came too. We played word games in teams and fed them sugar.

'Miss has had a goitre, Sir,' said the girl whose grandfather has one. 'She pretends she hasn't.'

I knew Jim would correct her. But he said, 'Oh yes, I know about her goitre.'

The Smuts squeezed the entire school into the hall for a final assembly. The caretakers had removed all the chairs. We stood like packed skittles while Adrain spat into the microphone then sent us for an extra break, earning himself the loudest applause we could manage with trapped arms.

Period 4 was school tidy-up. On the lunch bell, we released the pupils. They disappeared like air from a balloon let go.

Bahlul, Jim, Sally and I bagged a table for the staff presentations. We accepted a hot dog and salad, and the austerity ration of Prosecco that Adrain dribbled into our glasses. Bahlul told us that he's asked the Smuts if he can work part-time next year. 'They agreed,' he said, 'within three seconds.'

I brought him up to date with my news and said, 'So you and I might end up job-sharing.'

Jim nudged him. 'Bahlul, she said *sharing.*'

Sally said, shyly, 'Well, if I get the Head of Department post, I'll be keeping tabs on you *all.*'

We stared. She looked tearful but calm. 'The wedding's kind of postponed,' she said. She bit her lip. 'So – so I'll need something else to focus on.'

'Sally,' I said, but couldn't find any more words.

'Well, wish me luck for the interview, everyone,' she said, 'or I'll think you don't want me.'

Jim picked up his glass. 'Let's raise our meagre thimbleful of fizz and toast the new boss.'

'Premature!' Sally said.

He winked. 'I have my sources.'

We clinked our glasses. Bahlul said to Sally, 'Will you still bring cake?'

Jim gave him a shove.

A humid night. Sat in the garden with Spouse after dinner until the birds quietened.

Have ordered a summer-weight duvet to help with the sweats.

Acknowledgements

I'm indebted to English teacher Mr Jackson, who taught me at Kenilworth Grammar School, Warwickshire, in the 1970s and inspired my own decision to teach English. I've tried to trace him without success, but he avoided me in corridors even then.

Another teacher, the late Colin Archer, ran creative writing classes in the 1990s at Surrey Adult Education. Colin, I promised I'd acknowledge you should I ever be published, and I'm so sorry you're not around to see your name. Thank you for telling me the bald truth about all the '-ing' words and the overdone similes.

I'll also thank my family for their support and longsuffering, those mentioned in the book and those not mentioned in the interests of economy and simplicity. Thanks and apologies to Paul (Spouse) for, well, let's not dwell.

Thank you, Deborah Jenkins, close friend and fellow-writer-in-anguish, for all your feedback on my writing over the years and for your encouragement and belief in me.

Thank you to everyone in the Association of Christian Writers. I count many of you as friends. Your continual support, encouragement, celebration of success and commiseration after rejections have been appreciated.

I must thank Jonathan Davidson at Writing West Midlands. My selection for the 2016/17 Room 204 emerging writers' mentoring programme was a turning point. Jonathan, we sat in that café in Leamington and while I tried to work out how a twenty-first-century teapot operated, you told me that funny writing can be tragic and tragic writing can be funny and to ignore any fool who says it can't.

Many thanks to the nice people at Warwick Printing who gave me free advice via LiveChat about producing school magazines, even though my magazine was only to be fictional and therefore non-remunerative for them.

I'd like to acknowledge the influence of Sylvia Plath's poem 'Mirror', which is about a mirror that feels miffed at the grumpy responses of the ageing woman who looks into it daily. I love the poem and have used it many times in lessons to prove that inanimate objects such as mirrors, fridges and front doors have feelings and opinions. Plath didn't write a poem called 'Bathroom Scales', unfortunately, but you can't have everything.

Last but not least, huge appreciation is due to all the lovely people at SPCK who have commissioned, edited, marketed and promoted this book. Particular thanks go to Tony Collins, who first suggested I write a funny memoir based in a school and then championed it when I finally came round to the idea.

WE HAVE A VISION
OF A WORLD IN
WHICH EVERYONE IS
TRANSFORMED BY
CHRISTIAN KNOWLEDGE

As well as being an award-winning publisher, SPCK is the oldest Anglican mission agency in the world.

Our mission is to lead the way in creating books and resources that help everyone to make sense of faith.

Will you partner with us to put good books into the hands of prisoners, great assemblies in front of schoolchildren and reach out to people who have not yet been touched by the Christian faith?

To donate, please visit www.spckpublishing.co.uk/donate or call our friendly fundraising team on 020 7592 3900.